This is a great resource for the study of biblical languages. The definitions will help students, and the examples will reinforce their meaning and significance. I wish I had this resource when I began my studies.

> MILES V. VAN PELT, The Alan Hayes Belcher Jr. Professor of
> Old Testament and Biblical Languages and academic dean
> at Reformed Theological Seminary in Jackson, Mississippi

It's a strange but common phenomenon that the grammatically impoverished state of English speakers is a major challenge for them in learning Greek and Hebrew. Several books have attempted to address this problem, but I know of no text that addresses key English grammatical concepts as skillfully and comprehensively as Kyle Greenwood's handy book. Pastors who consult the best technical biblical commentaries (and sometimes find themselves befuddled by the grammatical terminology) will also find this to be a useful resource.

> ROBERT L. PLUMMER, Collin and Eveyln Aikman Professor of
> Biblical Studies, The Southern Baptist Theological Seminary

Kyle Greenwood has produced an invaluable tool that all students and professors will want to have as a resource in teaching and learning biblical languages. This volume could even help non-Greek and Hebrew students when using commentaries and tools that assume knowledge of these terms. I intend to use this in my own seminary Greek courses I teach. Highly recommended.

> DAVID MATHEWSON, associate professor of
> New Testament, Denver Seminary

With a blend of technical data, accessible explanations, and specific textual examples, Greenwood provides the missing ingredient in many students' Hebrew and Greek study: ready descriptions of the basic grammatical features of English and their relevance for the biblical languages. This book is a first-rate classroom resource that is eminently usable with its alphabetical order of entries and concrete biblical examples. It will serve both students and teachers of the biblical languages.

> BRAD E. KELLE, professor of Old
> Hebrew, Point Loma Nazarene

Dictionary of English Grammar for Students of Biblical Languages is an exceptional and much-needed resource that addresses the gap between students' grasp of English grammatical concepts and assumptions that grammars and professors often make about students' prior knowledge. Not only does the dictionary offer highly understandable definitions for each grammatical term, it also provides easy-to-grasp English examples and, when relevant, helpful Greek and Hebrew illustrations. This dictionary will prove to be an indispensable asset for students and professors of biblical languages alike.

> NICK ELDER, visiting assistant professor of New Testament,
> University of Dubuque Theological Seminary

Robust enough for advanced students but readable enough for beginners, Greenwood's *A Dictionary of English Grammar for Students of Biblical Languages* is immensely practical. It anticipates student hang-ups and questions and offers sensible advice for navigating biblical languages. Rather than guessing, students can use this book to quickly get up to speed on grammatical terms. Examples are clear and useful for the classroom, and I'm delighted to recommend it to my students.

> CARMEN JOY IMES, associate professor of
> Old Testament, Prairie College

It is hard enough to learn biblical languages. But it becomes nearly impossible for students who lack sufficient background in elementary language concepts. This volume helpfully defines the most important concepts and illustrates them with numerous examples. The dictionary will no doubt fill a need for many students, who will want to have Greenwood's volume nearby during their first year of language study.

> BILL T. ARNOLD, Paul S. Amos Professor of Old Testament
> Interpretation, Asbury Theological Seminary

DICTIONARY
OF English Grammar
FOR STUDENTS OF
BIBLICAL LANGUAGES

DICTIONARY
OF English Grammar
FOR STUDENTS OF
BIBLICAL LANGUAGES

KYLE GREENWOOD

ZONDERVAN ACADEMIC

ZONDERVAN ACADEMIC

Dictionary of English Grammar for Students of Biblical Languages
Copyright © 2020 by Kyle Greenwood

Requests for information should be addressed to:
Zondervan, *3900 Sparks Dr. SE, Grand Rapids, Michigan 49546*

ISBN 978-0-310-09844-7 (softcover)

Cover design: Holli Leegwater
Interior design: Kait Lamphere

Printed in the United States of America

HB 08.05.2024

To Mom and Dad,
who imparted to me the English language,
instilled in me the rules of grammar,
ingrained in me the value of being a student,
and inspired in me a love for the Bible.

CONTENTS

INTRODUCTION

One summer many years ago I lived in Nairobi, Kenya. It was the first time I needed a passport to travel and the first time I left the North American continent. As a naive young man, I was surprised to learn that most Kenyans spoke at least five languages. As remarkable as that seemed to me at the time, it is more remarkable to me now how many native English-speaking Americans are only monolingual. Sure, many college-bound American students will take a few semesters of a foreign language in high school, but for the most part they simply do not have the wide exposure to languages to feel comfortable with them . . . especially if those languages are dead!

Learning a new language, even one's mother tongue, takes time, effort, exposure, and repetition. Notice how often young children are corrected with respect to subject-verb agreement, proper pronunciation, and appropriate vocabulary.

Little Johnny: "We go church."

Mother: "That's right, Johnny. We *are going to* church."

If it takes three to five years of complete language immersion to get a grasp on a first language, consider the challenges of learning a biblical language with only a few hours of engagement per week. It is no wonder that many students become petrified with the prospect. And it is unsurprising that students with only six credit hours of a biblical language only "know enough to be dangerous."

If learning a new alphabet, vocabulary, and syntax isn't bad enough for students of biblical languages, there's another type of language with its own vocabulary that is often lacking on the part of students but assumed by professors—the language of English grammar. Many students often say that the first time they learned English grammar was when they took a foreign language course. Students know how to *use* the English language (maybe not perfectly, but certainly functionally), but they have no idea how to describe the grammatical features and functions of their native tongue. This is often no fault of their own. With limited time and resources, English grammar has had to take a back seat to other important subjects. As an educator this reality is tough to admit, but knowing the laws and lexicon of English grammar isn't necessary to succeed in life. One can have a long and prosperous career as an accountant or zoologist without knowing the difference between a pronoun and a preposition. But it *is* necessary to succeed in the study of biblical languages.

Unfortunately, too many students of biblical languages *don't* know the difference between a pronoun and a preposition. To exasperate matters, too many professors don't realize this fact, or simply don't have time in an already rushed semester to address this language barrier. This leaves the student having to figure it out on their own (on top of the time they should be spending studying the actual Hebrew or Greek) or the professor hoping the students will inductively catch on with enough repetition of this foreign vocabulary.

This *Dictionary of English Grammar for Students of Biblical Languages* was designed to address this very need that most students and professors of biblical languages face. Professors would like to have more time in class to talk about the grammar, syntax, and vocabulary of Hebrew and Greek. Students would like to have a resource to turn to when the professor uses vocabulary she assumes the student would know and understand.

—— FORMAT ——

Dictionary of English Grammar for Students of Biblical Languages includes over 150 entries of grammatical terms, listed in alphabetical order. Where necessary, I have attempted to define the term according to its specific uses in English, Hebrew, and Greek. Since some grammarians or instructors use different terms for the same idea, I have tried to include all pertinent terms in the list of entries, with undefined cross-listings to help the reader more easily locate the term for which they are searching. With nearly every defined term, I provide three biblical examples to illustrate how that grammatical feature functions in context, followed by a brief explanation of the feature in that context. The first example will come from the English Bible, the second from the Hebrew Bible (followed by an English translation), and the third will come from the Greek New Testament (also followed by an English translation). Each of the examples are catalogued in the Scripture index at the end of the book for quick reference. In a very few cases, where the term is specific to only one of the biblical languages, I define the term and provide an example in that language alone. In other cases, I do not give any examples; instead, I direct the reader to a more generic entry that covers both languages. In addition to the aforementioned Scripture index, I have also included a bibliography of resources for further study of the biblical languages.

Here I should say a brief word about broad categories of terms in which some discretion was required regarding their inclusion or exclusion from the dictionary. One such category has to do with degrees of precision. There are numerous types of clauses, sentences, verbs, and other grammatical categories. Beside it being impractical to list, define, and provide examples for each, it is also important to keep in mind that many subcategories are somewhat arbitrary, such that grammarians themselves are not in full agreement on which subcategory, if any, a particular term should belong. For this reason, I have tried to be as specific as possible with terms without including so many that it reaches the point of absurdity. Another such category pertains to nongrammatical literary features, such as morphology or rhetorical devices. There is sometimes a fine line separating these categories. For example, *parallelism* is a rhetorical device found primarily in Hebrew poetry, but it is not altogether absent of grammatical meaning since it affects how one line of poetry relates to another line of poetry. However, there are more precise grammatical terms to explain those relationships. By contrast, *ellipsis* is similarly a type of rhetorical device, also found predominantly in poetry, but it has been included since the grammatical function related to it is unique. Furthermore, I have included a handful of terms that are not grammatical terms per se but are fundamental to any discussion on the subject. For these terms, I have marked them with an asterisk (*) and have defined them, but I do not provide any examples. In short, I used my best judgment, flawed as it may be, in determining which entries best serve the overall purpose of the book in assisting students of biblical languages with English grammar terminology.

—— TRANSLATION ——

Anyone who has ever translated from one language to another knows there is no such thing as a "literal" translation. We can translate words precisely from one language to the next, but those same words take on a different meaning in a different cultural context. We must take into consideration not only *what* the words mean, but *how* they mean. Ask any married couple if the words themselves are necessary to convey the intent of their message! Or, take for example, the Spanish phrase *hasta la vista*. A "literal" translation, "until the sighting," makes little sense in most cases. But what it *means* is "goodbye" (followed by "baby," of course, if you're about to shoot a liquid-nitrogen-frozen T-1000).

If translation is challenging between two modern languages, like Spanish and English, imagine the hurdles we face when moving from a dead language (Hebrew or Greek) to a living language (English).

There are scores of modern English translations of the Bible, each attempting to say with a little more clarity what the translators believe is most faithful to the original text. On one end of the spectrum are "formal equivalent" translations; that is, they attempt to maintain the same "form" as the original language, keeping the same word order as much as possible and attempting to translate one Hebrew or Greek word with the same English word at every occurrence. Formal equivalent translations require work on the part of the reader to determine the meanings of idioms and to get the general sense of the passage. On the other end of the spectrum are "functional equivalent" translations; that is, they endeavor to convey the thoughts and ideas of the original languages into a modern setting, even if that means changing vocabulary and sentence structure altogether. Functional equivalent translations make most of the interpretive decisions for the readers. As a spectrum suggests, there are many points between these two extremities.

In a resource like this one, it is important for a translation to lie somewhere between the two ends of the spectrum. A translation too formal makes for stilted reading and misses some grammatical features. A translation too functional, while offering more readable prose, misses a larger swath of grammatical features.

Having tested several of the more popular translations against a sample of various grammatical terms, I found that the NRSV provided the best balance of formality with a high correspondence of Hebrew/Greek to English vocabulary, as well as functionality that takes into account the manner in which grammatical features operate in the sentence. This is not to say that the NRSV is perfect, or even ideal, for every entry in the *Dictionary*. However, for the purposes of this book, it required the least additional commentary to explain the English in light of the Hebrew or Greek.

—— AUDIENCE ——

This *Dictionary of English Grammar* is intended to function as a collateral textbook, serving alongside other assigned textbooks for a course in Biblical Hebrew or Greek. It is not meant to replace the primary grammar textbook, nor is it meant to be read cover to cover. Rather, I envision this book being used as a reference by students (and professors, to some extent) to consult when the student needs a definition, an explanation, or clarification regarding specific grammatical terms. If, for example, a student does not know the difference between a pronoun and a preposition, the student could refer to the dictionary for clarification. Similarly, a professor can deflect questions related to grammatical terms, sending students to learn and study on their own, saving valuable class time for more substantive issues. Instructors may benefit from the *Dictionary* as well, as a quick reference for definitions and examples. Instructors who do not teach biblical languages often will benefit from the book as a refresher in grammatical terminology.

The book was designed primarily with first-year students of Biblical Hebrew or Greek in mind. (Due to the small corpus and equally small student population in biblical Aramaic courses, I have regrettably omitted that biblical language from this reference work.) Typically these are the students who will most struggle with learning a new biblical language, on the one hand, while becoming frustrated with terminology from a language they are supposed to already know, on the other. Furthermore, reading the corresponding examples will inevitably introduce them to new vocabulary items or present familiar vocabulary in a biblical context. However, the book will also benefit intermediate students and beyond. First, save for the most grammatical savvy among us, grammatical terminology is not second nature to most. Second, many entries in the dictionary are not everyday terms. Seasoned grammatical veterans confuse terms on occasion.

In either case, having ready access to the dictionary could prove valuable. Third, intermediate and advanced students can use the examples to brush up on their skills in the biblical languages. With nearly a hundred examples in each language—Hebrew, Greek, and English—there are plenty of opportunities for practice and refinement.

—— SOURCES ——

It probably goes without saying that there have been many influences throughout the years on the content of this book—elementary-school teachers, graduate-school professors, students, colleagues, and dozens of Greek and Hebrew grammar textbooks. My thinking on grammatical issues has no doubt been shaped in some way by all these forces in my life. Although the definitions featured in this book are my own, there are only so many ways to describe certain grammatical terms. As such, despite my best efforts to be creatively unique throughout, there will at times appear to be borrowing from one or many sources. It is the unfortunate reality of a work like this. Futhermore, I have gone to great lengths to use my own examples and illustrations. In a very few cases, however, examples from other sources have found their way into the book. This is somewhat inevitable, given the limited corpus of the biblical material. However, in those instances any commentary and discussion surrounding them are purely my own.

DICTIONARY

— **A** —

ABLATIVE CASE: The ablative case expresses the idea of separation and is seen by many grammarians as a subset of the genitive case. In Greek, substantives of separation carry the genitive case ending. See *Case*; *Genitive case*.

ABSOLUTE PHRASE: An absolute phrase lacks a finite verb, typically begins with a participle, and provides useful but unnecessary information about the subject of the independent clause. Normally set apart with a comma, an absolute phrase could be removed from the sentence without the sentence losing any essential meaning. Example: His hand fatigued from incessant writing, Matthew dropped his pencil onto the floor. Due to the particular nuances of the Hebrew participle, there are no certain attestations of the absolute phrase in the Hebrew Bible. The Greek genitive absolute does not correspond directly with the absolute phrase in English grammar; rather, it is a participial phrase that functions as a subordinate clause. See also *Genitive absolute*; *Participle*; *Phrase*; *Subordinate clause*.

ABSTRACT NOUN: An abstract noun refers to a concept, idea, or quality. In contrast to a concrete noun, an abstract noun cannot be identified by one of the five senses. See also *Concrete noun*; *Noun*.

EXAMPLES:

1. The fear of the Lᴏʀᴅ is the beginning of wisdom,
    and the knowledge of the Holy One is insight. (Prov 9:10)

    • The instructions of Proverbs 1–9 conclude with an appeal to four abstract nouns: fear, wisdom, knowledge, and insight, each of which expresses an intangible concept.

2.   הוֹדוּ לַיהוָה כִּי־טוֹב כִּי לְעוֹלָם חַסְדּוֹ׃

    O give thanks to the Lᴏʀᴅ, for he is good,
        for his steadfast love endures forever. (Ps 136:1)

- Each of the twenty-six verses of Psalm 136 carries the refrain "his steadfast love endures forever" (לְעוֹלָם חַסְדּוֹ). The Hebrew word translated as "steadfast love" (חֶסֶד) is an abstract noun as it cannot be identified by one of the five senses.

3. νυνὶ δὲ μένει πίστις, ἐλπίς, ἀγάπη, τὰ τρία ταῦτα· μείζων δὲ τούτων ἡ ἀγάπη.

And now faith, hope, and love abide, these three; and the greatest of these is love. (1 Cor 13:13).

- Paul's famous chapter on love concludes by listing three abstract nouns: "faith" (πίστις), "hope" (ἐλπίς), and "love" (ἀγάπη), the greatest of which, Paul declares is ἀγάπη.

*ACCENT: Accent refers to the syllable in the word on which the stress is placed. Where the accent is placed often affects how the syllable is pronounced. Therefore, in some cases the position of the accent can change the meaning of a word. For example, *conflict* (KAHN-flikt) is a noun meaning "a battle or disagreement," while *conflict* (kən-FLIKT) is a verb meaning "to be incompatible."

ACCUSATIVE CASE: The accusative case of a noun is the case used to identify the direct object of a verb. English does not have a means of indicating the accusative case other than its function and position within the sentence. Greek nouns have case endings, which vary depending on gender, number, and declension. In Semitic languages the accusative case was originally represented by the *-a(m)* suffix, as seen in Akkadian and Ugaritic. Hebrew nouns originally had case endings, which have mostly been lost. Instead, Biblical Hebrew uses the particle אֵת as the definite direct object marker and is called in some grammars the sign of the accusative.[1] Some verbs are

---

1. There are instances in Biblical Hebrew in which אֵת follows a passive verb; therefore, it cannot be a marker of the accusative. In this light, some grammarians prefer to see this particle as simply an emphatic indicator of definiteness.

governed by certain prepositions (primarily בְּ), which are affixed to the accusative noun. Vestiges of the accusative are found in some archaic words and in some forms (perhaps, e.g., the directional ה-, as in אַרְצָה ["toward the land" or "land-ward"]). However, in Semitic languages it might be best to speak of an "adverbial case" rather than an "accusative case." See also *Adverbial accusative*; *Case*; *Direct object*.

EXAMPLES:

1. Moses was keeping the flock of his father-in-law Jethro, the priest of Midian; he led his flock beyond the wilderness, and came to Horeb, the mountain of God. (Exod 3:1)

    • Although English does not have case endings to mark their grammatical function in the sentence, the noun "flock" functions as an accusative in both of its uses, serving as the direct object of the verbs "was keeping" and "led."

2. וּבֶן־הֲדַד מֶלֶךְ־אֲרָם קָבַץ אֶת־כָּל־חֵילוֹ וּשְׁלֹשִׁים וּשְׁנַיִם מֶלֶךְ אִתּוֹ וְסוּס וָרָכֶב וַיַּעַל וַיָּצַר עַל־שֹׁמְרוֹן וַיִּלָּחֶם בָּהּ:

    King Ben-hadad of Aram gathered all his army together; thirty-two kings were with him, along with horses and chariots. He marched against Samaria, laid siege to it, and attacked it. (1 Kgs 20:1)

    • Although not indicated morphologically, "all his army" (כָּל־חֵילוֹ) is in the accusative case, as indicated by the definite direct object marker, אֶת־. The final verb of the verse, "and attacked" (וַיִּלָּחֶם) also takes an accusative, in this case the third feminine singular pronoun הּ- ("it"), which is governed by the inseparable preposition בְּ.

3. ἐνδύσασθε τὴν πανοπλίαν τοῦ Θεοῦ πρὸς τὸ δύνασθαι ὑμᾶς στῆναι πρὸς τὰς μεθοδείας τοῦ διαβόλου.

    Put on the whole armor of God, so that you may be able to stand against the wiles of the devil. (Eph 6:11)

- Since Greek utilizes case endings, it is easy to identify the accusative noun in Ephesians 6:11, which follows the imperative "put on" (ἐνδύσασθε), indicating that what one should put on is "the whole armor" (τὴν πανοπλίαν).

ACTIVE VOICE: In the active voice, the subject performs an action on another noun. In Greek, the active voice is identified morphologically within the verbal form. In Hebrew, voice may be indicated by the stem (typically Qal, Piel, and Hiphil), as well as morphology. See also *Voice.*

EXAMPLES:

1. In the beginning when God created the heavens and the earth, the earth was a formless void and darkness covered the face of the deep, while a wind from God swept over the face of the waters. (Gen 1:1–2)

   - God is the actor of the creation event. God is not being acted on but is acting *on* "the heavens and earth." The verb "created" is in the active voice.

2. וַיִּקַּח שְׁמוּאֵל אֶת־קֶרֶן הַשֶּׁמֶן וַיִּמְשַׁח אֹתוֹ בְּקֶרֶב אֶחָיו

   Then Samuel took the horn of oil, and anointed him in the presence of his brothers. (1 Sam 16:13a)

   - The verbs "took" (וַיִּקַּח) and "anointed" (וַיִּמְשַׁח) are in the Qal stem and are in the active voice. Samuel (שְׁמוּאֵל) produces the action of taking "the horn of oil" (אֶת־קֶרֶן הַשֶּׁמֶן) and anointing "him" (אֹתוֹ), a third masculine singular pronominal suffix on the sign of the accusative אֵת.

3. Καὶ εἰσῆλθεν Ἰησοῦς εἰς τὸ ἱερὸν καὶ ἐξέβαλεν πάντας τοὺς πωλοῦντας καὶ ἀγοράζοντας ἐν τῷ ἱερῷ, καὶ τὰς τραπέζας τῶν κολλυβιστῶν κατέστρεψεν καὶ τὰς καθέδρας τῶν πωλούντων τὰς περιστεράς

   Then Jesus entered the temple and drove out all who were selling and buying in the temple, and he overturned the tables of the money changers and the seats of those who sold doves. (Matt 21:12)

- In this dramatic passage, Jesus acts on three different objects. First, he "entered" (εἰσῆλθεν) "the temple" (τὸ ἱερόν). Next he "drove out" (ἐξέβαλεν) all who were selling and buying. Third, he "overturned" (κατέστρεψεν) "the tables" (τὰς τραπέζας) and "the seats" (τὰς καθέδρας) of those same people. Students of Greek will also recognize these forms as being in the active voice from their morphological construction.

ADJECTIVE: An adjective is a word that describes or modifies a noun. Moreover, both biblical languages have three types of adjectives: attributive, predicate, and substantive. See *Attributive adjective*; *Predicate adjective*; *Substantival adjective*.

ADVERB: An adverb is a word that describes or modifies verbs, adjectives, or other adverbs. Examples of English adverbs include *here*, *now*, *quite*, *well*, and words ending in -*ly* (e.g., *gently*, *diligently*). There are five basic types of adverbs: adverbs of degree (how much), frequency (how often), manner (how), time (when), and place (where).

EXAMPLES:

1. Then the LORD said to me, "Get up, go down quickly from here, for your people whom you have brought from Egypt have acted corruptly. They have been quick to turn from the way that I commanded them; they have cast an image for themselves." (Deut 9:12)

   - "Quickly" is an adverb of manner, describing the way in which God wanted Moses to come down from Mt. Sinai.

2. וַיְהִי בְּנָסְעָם מִקֶּדֶם וַיִּמְצְאוּ בִקְעָה בְּאֶרֶץ שִׁנְעָר וַיֵּשְׁבוּ שָׁם׃

   And as they migrated from the east, they came upon a plain in the land of Shinar and settled there. (Gen 11:2)

   - The adverb "there" (שָׁם) is an adverb of place, describing the location of where they settled (וַיֵּשְׁבוּ).

3. εὐθὺς κράξας ὁ πατὴρ τοῦ παιδίου ἔλεγεν, Πιστεύω βοήθει μου τῇ ἀπιστίᾳ.

Immediately the father of the child cried out, "I believe; help my unbelief!" (Mark 9:24)

- The adverb "immediately" (εὐθύς) is an adverb of time, expressing when the "father of the child" (ὁ πατὴρ τοῦ παιδίου) "cried out" (κράξας).

ADVERBIAL ACCUSATIVE: An adverbial accusative is a noun form in the accusative case, modifying the circumstances under which the action of the verb occurs. These circumstances may pertain to place, time, manner, or state, to name a few. Adverbial accusatives could be translated by adding the *-ly* ending, but they often require a preposition to smooth out the translation. Due to this often necessary addition of a preposition, English examples are rare. See also *Adverb*; *Accusative case*; *Nominative*.

EXAMPLES:

1. וַיֹּאמֶר יְהוֹשֻׁעַ מֶה עֲכַרְתָּנוּ יַעְכָּרְךָ יְהוָה בַּיּוֹם הַזֶּה וַיִּרְגְּמוּ אֹתוֹ כָל־יִשְׂרָאֵל אֶבֶן וַיִּשְׂרְפוּ אֹתָם בָּאֵשׁ וַיִּסְקְלוּ אֹתָם בָּאֲבָנִים: וַיָּקִימוּ עָלָיו גַּל־אֲבָנִים גָּדוֹל עַד הַיּוֹם הַזֶּה

Joshua said, "Why did you bring trouble on us? The LORD is bringing trouble on you today." And all Israel stoned him to death; they burned them with fire, cast stones on them, and raised over him a great heap of stones that remains to this day. (Josh 7:25–26a)

- The phrase translated "stoned him to death" more rigidly reads, "killed him stonily"; that is, they killed him *with* stones. The noun "stone" (אֶבֶן) is an example of an adverbial accusative of manner.

2. καὶ ἔζησαν καὶ ἐβασίλευσαν μετὰ τοῦ Χριστοῦ χίλια ἔτη.

They came to life and reigned with Christ a thousand years. (Rev 20:4)

- The phrase "a thousand years" (χίλια ἔτη) is comprised of a noun and adjective in the accusative case. The phrase behaves as an adverb of time, describing the duration of Christ's reign.

AGENT: The noun that conducts the action of a passive verb is known as the agent of the verb. Agency is often indicated by a prepositional phrase, such as "with fire" or "by the edge of the sword." In the Bible, agency is often implied rather than stated explicitly. When God is the implied agent, this is referred to as *divine agency*. See also *Passive voice*.

EXAMPLES:

1. John would have prevented him, saying, "I need to be baptized by you, and do you come to me?" (Matt 3:14)

   - John protested Jesus's requests for John to baptize him. The passive verb "be baptized" required an agent, which in this case is "you," referring to Jesus. Note the use of the preposition "by" to complete the construction.

2.

אַשְׁרֶיךָ יִשְׂרָאֵל מִי כָמוֹךָ
עַם נוֹשַׁע בַּיהוָה
מָגֵן עֶזְרֶךָ
וַאֲשֶׁר־חֶרֶב גַּאֲוָתֶךָ
וְיִכָּחֲשׁוּ אֹיְבֶיךָ לָךְ
וְאַתָּה עַל־בָּמוֹתֵימוֹ תִדְרֹךְ׃

Happy are you, O Israel! Who is like you,
    a people saved by the LORD,
the shield of your help,
    and the sword of your triumph!
Your enemies shall come fawning to you,
    and you shall tread on their backs. (Deut 33:29)

   - The verb "saved" (נוֹשַׁע) is a Niphal perfect in the passive voice. The agent of the verb is indicated by the prepositional phrase "by the LORD" (בַּיהוָה). That is, the LORD is the one doing the saving. This is an example of divine agency.

3. μηδεὶς πειραζόμενος λεγέτω ὅτι ἀπὸ θεοῦ πειράζομαι· ὁ γὰρ θεὸς ἀπείραστός ἐστιν κακῶν, πειράζει δὲ αὐτὸς οὐδένα.

No one, when tempted, should say, "I am being tempted by God"; for God cannot be tempted by evil and he himself tempts no one. (Jas 1:13)

• The verb "being tempted" (πειράζομαι) is in the passive mood, requiring an agent. The divine agent is indicated by the prepositional phrase "by God" (ἀπὸ θεοῦ).

AKTIONSART: Aktionsart refers to a verb's action with respect to time. A verb that has a beginning, duration, and end (e.g., "ate") is said to be a telic verb, describing an action that is complete. A verb that only has a duration (e.g., "eating") is said to be an atelic verb, describing an action that is incomplete. Both Hebrew and Greek express aktionsart by virtue of the verbal tense and its context. See *Aspect*; *Tense*.

ANARTHROUS: See *Article*; *Definiteness*.

ANTECEDENT: The antecedent is a word, phrase, event, or clause to which a particular pronoun refers. The antecedent always precedes the pronoun and is generally the thing nearest to the pronoun. Sometimes the antecedent is one or more sentences removed from the pronoun.

EXAMPLES:

1. "For God so loved the world that he gave his only Son, so that everyone who believes in him may not perish but may have eternal life." (John 3:16)

• God is the antecedent for both "he" and "his." Son is the antecedent for "him."

2.

וַיִּבְרָא אֱלֹהִים אֶת־הָאָדָם בְּצַלְמוֹ
בְּצֶלֶם אֱלֹהִים בָּרָא אֹתוֹ
זָכָר וּנְקֵבָה בָּרָא אֹתָם:

So God created humankind in his image,
   in the image of God he created them;
   male and female he created them. (Gen 1:27)

- Genesis 1:27 breaks the rule of proximity on two counts.
  First, the nearest referent to "his" is "humankind" (הָאָדָם),
  but the antecedent is clearly "God" (אֱלֹהִים) as indicated by the
  parallel phrase "in the image of God" (בְּצֶלֶם אֱלֹהִים). Second,
  even though "God" is the nearest referent for "them" (אֹתוֹ),
  the antecedent must be "humankind" as the object of God's
  creative act. This passage indicates that even though rules of
  syntax are helpful in determining the antecedent of a pronoun,
  context must be taken into account.

3. ὁ δὲ ἔφη, Ἄνδρες ἀδελφοὶ καὶ πατέρες, ἀκούσατε. Ὁ θεὸς τῆς
   δόξης ὤφθη τῷ πατρὶ ἡμῶν Ἀβραὰμ ὄντι ἐν τῇ Μεσοποταμίᾳ
   πρὶν ἢ κατοικῆσαι αὐτὸν ἐν Χαρράν. . . . Ἀκούοντες δὲ ταῦτα
   διεπρίοντο ταῖς καρδίαις αὐτῶν καὶ ἔβρυχον τοὺς ὀδόντας ἐπ᾽
   αὐτόν.

And Stephen [lit., "he"] replied: "Brothers and fathers, listen to me. The God
of glory appeared to our ancestor Abraham when he was in Mesopotamia,
before he lived in Haran. . . ." When they heard these things, they became
enraged and ground their teeth at Stephen [lit., "him"]. (Acts 7:2, 54)

- Acts 7:54 exemplifies two less-common features of antecedents.
  First, the antecedent of "these things" (ταῦτα) is the entirety
  of Stephen's discourse (Acts 7:2–53), demonstrating that an
  antecedent need not be a single noun. Second, the antecedent
  for both "they" (αὐτῶν) and "him" (αὐτόν) in Acts 7:54 is
  Stephen and appears a full sixty verses earlier in Acts 6:9!

APODOSIS: In a conditional sentence, the apodosis states the result
of the condition, generally marked in English by the adverb *then*,
although it is often unnecessary. In Hebrew, the apodosis is typically
marked by the conjunctive *waw*, though it is not required. In Greek,

the apodosis is not usually marked with a specific lexeme, except in second-class conditions (contrary to fact), in which the apodosis is introduced by ἄν. In English translations, "then" is often implied and is left untranslated. See also *Conditional sentence*; *Protasis*.

EXAMPLES:

1. "If you know me, you will know my Father also. From now on you do know him and have seen him." (John 14:7)

   • The conditional sentence begins with the protasis, "if you know me." The result of that condition is that "you will know my Father also," the apodosis of the conditional sentence. In the Greek, the apodosis is introduced by καὶ, which has been left untranslated in the NRSV, as it is unnecessary to make sense of the sentence.

2. אִם־כֶּסֶף תַּלְוֶה אֶת־עַמִּי אֶת־הֶעָנִי עִמָּךְ לֹא־תִהְיֶה לוֹ כְּנֹשֶׁה לֹא־תְשִׂימוּן עָלָיו נֶשֶׁךְ׃

   If you lend money to my people, to the poor among you, you shall not deal with them as a creditor; you shall not exact interest from them. (Exod 22:25 [22:24 MT]).

   • The apodosis of the conditional sentence is the twofold prohibition, "you shall not deal with them as a creditor; you shall not exact interest from them" לֹא־תִהְיֶה לוֹ כְּנֹשֶׁה לֹא־תְשִׂימוּן עָלָיו נֶשֶׁךְ). The result of lending money should not be one of dishonest gain. Therefore, the apodosis entails a prohibition against unjust business dealings.

3. Εἴ τις οὖν παράκλησις ἐν Χριστῷ, εἴ τι παραμύθιον ἀγάπης, εἴ τις κοινωνία πνεύματος, εἴ τις σπλάγχνα καὶ οἰκτιρμοί, πληρώσατέ μου τὴν χαρὰν ἵνα τὸ αὐτὸ φρονῆτε, τὴν αὐτὴν ἀγάπην ἔχοντες, σύνψυχοι, τὸ ἓν φρονοῦντες

   If then there is any encouragement in Christ, any consolation from love, any sharing in the Spirit, any compassion and sympathy, make my joy complete: be of the same mind, having the same love, being in full accord and of one mind. (Phil 2:1–2)

- Philippians 2 begins with four conditions. Paul states that the result of the church in Philippi meeting each of the conditions is the imperatival clause, "make my joy complete" (πληρώσατέ μου τὴν χαρὰν), the apodosis of the conditional sentence.

APPOSITION: Apposition is a syntactic relationship between parallel or otherwise synonymous nouns or noun phrases that are situated consecutively in a sentence, clause, or phrase. The simple juxtaposition of words or phrases allows the second word or phrase in the sequence to further clarify the first word or phrase. In Hebrew the nouns will generally agree in gender, number, and definiteness. In Greek, the words in apposition typically agree in gender, number, and case. See also *Epexegetical clause*.

EXAMPLES:

1. Now the man knew his wife Eve, and she conceived and bore Cain, saying, "I have produced a man with the help of the LORD." (Gen 4:1)

   - Adam's wife had been given the name "Eve" in Genesis 3:20. The juxtaposition of Eve with the phrase "his wife" provides clarity regarding the identity of Adam's wife in Genesis 4:1. This wife is not a different wife but the same one to whom the reader has already been introduced.

2. וּדְבוֹרָה אִשָּׁה נְבִיאָה אֵשֶׁת לַפִּידוֹת הִיא שֹׁפְטָה אֶת־יִשְׂרָאֵל בָּעֵת הַהִיא׃

   At that time Deborah, a prophetess, wife of Lappidoth, was judging Israel. (Judg 4:4)

   - The third judge of Israel is introduced by a series of appositional words and phrases, each agreeing in gender (fem.) and number (sg.) with Deborah, but not necessarily definiteness. The first word in apposition "a prophetess" is actually two in Hebrew, "a woman, a prophetess" (אִשָּׁה נְבִיאָה). Both "woman" (אִשָּׁה)

and "prophetess" (נְבִיאָה) agree with "Deborah" (דְּבוֹרָה) in gender and number, but not definiteness. Whereas "Deborah" is definite, "prophetess" is indefinite. Moreover, "the wife of Lappidoth" (אֵשֶׁת לַפִּידוֹת) also stands in apposition to "Deborah" and agrees with דְּבוֹרָה in gender, number, and definiteness.

3. Παῦλος δέσμιος Χριστοῦ Ἰησοῦ καὶ Τιμόθεος ὁ ἀδελφὸς Φιλήμονι τῷ ἀγαπητῷ καὶ συνεργῷ ἡμῶν

   Paul, a prisoner of Christ Jesus, and Timothy our brother, To Philemon our dear friend and co-worker. . . (Phlm 1)

   • There are several appositional words or phrases in this brief sentence. First, the phrase "a prisoner of Christ Jesus" (δέσμιος Χριστοῦ Ἰησοῦ) is in apposition to "Paul" (Παῦλος). Both Παῦλος and δέσμιος are nominative, masculine, singular nouns. Second, the noun phrase "our brother" [lit. "the brother"] (ὁ ἀδελφός) sits in apposition to "Timothy" (Τιμόθεος). Again, both Τιμόθεος and ὁ ἀδελφός are nominative, masculine, singular nouns. Finally, the phrase "our dear friend and co-worker" (τῷ ἀγαπητῷ καὶ συνεργῷ ἡμῶν) is in apposition to "Philemon" (Φιλήμονι). Since Philemon is the recipient of the letter, Φιλήμονι, τῷ ἀγαπητῷ, and συνεργῷ are all in the dative case.

ARTHROUS: See *Article*; *Definiteness*.

ARTICLE: An article is an adjective that defines the specificity of a noun. Something is said to be definite if it refers to one particular thing, while it is indefinite if it refers to any item in a category. In English, definite nouns are modified by the definite article *the*, while indefinite nouns are preceded by the indefinite articles *a* or *an*. Neither Hebrew nor Greek have indefinite articles. Words having an article are said to be "arthrous." Words lacking an article are said to be "anarthrous." See *Definiteness*.

ASPECT: Aspect denotes how the action of a verb is viewed from the perspective of an author or narrator. In Hebrew and Greek, aspect can be simplified as to whether an action is complete (perfective aspect) or incomplete (imperfective aspect). These two aspects are then expressed in the various tenses, but frequently they are not determined by strict verbal forms but by the context of the sentence. See *Imperfect tense*; *Perfect tense*; see also *Tense*.

ASYNDETIC CONSTRUCTION: An asyndectic construction occurs when a conjunction is omitted in a situation in which one would typically be used to join related elements in a sentence.

EXAMPLES:

1. The nations are in an uproar, the kingdoms totter;
   he utters his voice, the earth melts. (Ps 46:6)

   - As is typical in Hebrew poetry, certain elements are omitted and implied (called "gapping"; see *Ellipsis*). In this case, the missing element is the conjunction, which is also lacking in the Hebrew. Here we would expect a conjunction after each comma: "and kingdoms fall," "and the earth melts." Instead the second half of each line is in an asyndetic relationship with the first half of the corresponding line.

2.

מִי־זֹאת הַנִּשְׁקָפָה כְּמוֹ־שָׁחַר
יָפָה כַלְּבָנָה בָּרָה כַּחַמָּה
אֲיֻמָּה כַּנִּדְגָּלוֹת:

Who is this that looks forth like the dawn,
   fair as the moon, bright as the sun,
   terrible as an army with banners? (Song 6:10)

   - Song of Songs 6:10 is written in poetic verse structure. In a list of items or descriptions, normally a conjunction appears before the last item in the list. Since there is no conjunctive וְ separating the phrases "bright as the sun" (בָּרָה כַּחַמָּה) and "terrible as an army with banners" (אֲיֻמָּה כַּנִּדְגָּלוֹת), they are said to be in an asyndetic relationship.

3. ὅτε ἤμην νήπιος, ἐλάλουν ὡς νήπιος, ἐφρόνουν ὡς νήπιος, ἐλογιζόμην ὡς νήπιος· ὅτε γέγονα ἀνήρ, κατήργηκα τὰ τοῦ νηπίου.

When I was a child, I spoke like a child, I thought like a child, I reasoned like a child; when I became an adult, I put an end to childish ways. (1 Cor 13:11)

- The Greek demonstrates the asyndetic relationship between each of the clauses. Where a conjunction is expected before "I reasoned like a child" (ἐλογιζόμην ὡς νήπιος), the Greek is lacking one, creating an asyndetic construction.

ATELIC VERB: See *Aktionsart*.

ATTRIBUTIVE ADJECTIVE: An attributive adjective is a word that describes or further defines the noun it modifies. In Hebrew, the attributive adjective always follows the noun it modifies, and the two words must agree in gender, number, and definiteness. In Greek, the adjective and the noun it modifies must agree in case, gender, and number. However, the adjective may come before the noun (ascriptive position) or after the noun (restrictive position), but it will always follow the article if one is present. When the adjective stands between the article and the noun, it is sometimes called the "ascriptive" attributive position.

EXAMPLES:

1. The LORD is my shepherd, I shall not want.
   He makes me lie down in green pastures;
   he leads me beside still waters. (Ps 23:1–2)

   - "Green" and "still" ascribe an attribute to "pastures" and "waters," respectively. As is customary in English, such attributive adjectives precede the nouns they modify.

2. וַיהוָה הֵטִיל רוּחַ־גְּדוֹלָה אֶל־הַיָּם וַיְהִי סַעַר־גָּדוֹל בַּיָּם וְהָאֳנִיָּה חִשְּׁבָה
לְהִשָּׁבֵר:

But the LORD hurled a great wind upon the sea, and such a mighty storm came upon the sea that the ship threatened to break up. (Jonah 1:4)

- The adjective "great" (גָּדוֹל) appears twice in this verse, translated in the first instance as "great" and in the second instance as "mighty." In the first case, it modifies the noun "wind" (רוּחַ). Both the noun and attributive adjective are indefinite, singular, and feminine. In the second case, it modifies "storm" (סַעַר). Here, both the noun and attributive adjective are indefinite, singular, and masculine.

3. καὶ ἐξελθόντες ἐκ τῶν μνημείων μετὰ τὴν ἔγερσιν αὐτοῦ εἰσῆλθον εἰς τὴν ἁγίαν πόλιν καὶ ἐνεφανίσθησαν πολλοῖς.

After his resurrection they came out of the tombs and entered the holy city and appeared to many. (Matt 27:53)

- Matthew 27:53 provides an example of an attributive adjective in the first attributive position, in which the adjective is situated between the definite article and the noun it modifies. In this position, the adjective precedes the noun it modifies. Note that the feminine, singular, accusative adjective "holy" (ἁγίαν) follows the article "the" (τήν) and the noun "city" (πόλιν), both of which agree with the adjective in gender (fem.), number (sg.), and case (acc.).

4. Καὶ ἄλλος ἄγγελος ἦλθεν καὶ ἐστάθη ἐπὶ τοῦ θυσιαστηρίου ἔχων λιβανωτὸν χρυσοῦν, καὶ ἐδόθη αὐτῷ θυμιάματα πολλά, ἵνα δώσει ταῖς προσευχαῖς τῶν ἁγίων πάντων ἐπὶ τὸ θυσιαστήριον τὸ χρυσοῦν τὸ ἐνώπιον τοῦ θρόνου.

Another angel with a golden censer came and stood at the altar; he was given a great quantity of incense to offer with the prayers of all the saints on the golden altar that is before the throne. (Rev 8:3)

- The two uses of the adjective "golden" (χρυσοῦν) represent two examples of the restrictive attributive position, in which the adjective follows the noun and (if present) the article. In both instances, the adjective χρυσοῦς follows the noun it modifies and agrees with it in case, number, and gender. In the first case, χρυσοῦς modifies "censer" (λιβανωτός) and lacks the article. In the second case, χρυσοῦς modifies "altar" (θυσιαστήριον), and both the noun and the adjective are preceded by the article.

— B —

— C —

CARDINAL NUMBER: Cardinal numbers are those that are used for counting or to indicate the quantity of a set. Grammatically, cardinal numbers may be used substantivally or attributively. In Hebrew, cardinal numbers are governed by different grammatical rules, depending on the value of the number. Students should consult a Hebrew grammar for those rules. Cardinal numbers in Greek generally do not decline, with the exception of the number "one" (εἷς), which declines according to case and gender. For the nuances of the rules of declension for Greek cardinal numbers, students should refer to their Greek grammar textbook. In both Hebrew and Greek, cardinal numbers are often used symbolically or figuratively as well as literally.

EXAMPLES:

1. "But if you are not listened to, take one or two others along with you, so that every word may be confirmed by the evidence of two or three witnesses." (Matt 18:16)

- This verse contains the cardinal numbers "one," "two," and "three." The first set of numbers indicate the quantity of "others" who would go and speak to the offender. The last set of numbers indicates the quantity of witnesses available to confirm the conversation.

2. וַיִּחַר־אַף יְהוָה בְּיִשְׂרָאֵל וַיְנִעֵם בַּמִּדְבָּר אַרְבָּעִים שָׁנָה עַד־תֹּם כָּל־הַדּוֹר הָעֹשֶׂה הָרַע בְּעֵינֵי יְהוָה:

And the Lᴏʀᴅ's anger was kindled against Israel, and he made them wander in the wilderness for forty years, until all the generation that had done evil in the sight of the Lᴏʀᴅ had disappeared. (Num 32:13)

- This passage represents a case in which a cardinal number is likely used figuratively rather than to connote a precise number of years. In the Hebrew Bible the number "forty" (אַרְבָּעִים) often represents a generation, as is likely the case here. That is, the Israelites would wander in the wilderness until the present generation dies and the new generation matures. In any case, אַרְבָּעִים signifies the quantity of years Israel would spend in the wilderness.

3. Πίστει τὰ τείχη Ἰεριχὼ ἔπεσαν κυκλωθέντα ἐπὶ ἑπτὰ ἡμέρας.

By faith the walls of Jericho fell after they had been encircled for seven days. (Heb 11:30)

- The author of Hebrews recalls the story of Joshua 6 in which the Israelites marched around the city of Jericho "seven" (ἑπτά) days. The cardinal number qualifies how many days they marched.

CAUSAL CLAUSE: A causal clause is one that expresses the reason for a particular action. In English a causal clause typically begins with "because" or "for." Hebrew causal clauses are often introduced by the particle כִּי, while Greek causal clauses are most frequently introduced by ὅτι and γάρ. See also *Clause*; *Subordinate clause.*

Examples:

1. The man named his wife Eve, because she was the mother of all living. (Gen 3:20)

   - The reason the man named his wife Eve is given in the subordinate clause "because she was the mother of all living."

2.

   גַּם־בַּהֲמוֹת שָׂדֶה תַּעֲרוֹג אֵלֶיךָ
   כִּי יָבְשׁוּ אֲפִיקֵי מָיִם
   וְאֵשׁ אָכְלָה
   נְאוֹת הַמִּדְבָּר:

   Even the wild animals cry to you
      because the watercourses are dried up,
   and fire has devoured
      the pastures of the wilderness. (Joel 1:20)

   - The clause "because the watercourses are dried up" (כִּי יָבְשׁוּ אֲפִיקֵי מָיִם) is a causal clause expressing the rationale for why the wild animals cry out.

3. εἰ δὲ ὡς Χριστιανός, μὴ αἰσχυνέσθω, δοξαζέτω δὲ τὸν θεὸν ἐν τῷ ὀνόματι τούτῳ.

   Yet if any of you suffers as a Christian, do not consider it a disgrace, but glorify God because you bear this name. (1 Pet 4:16)

   - The clause "because you bear this name" (ἐν τῷ ὀνόματι τούτῳ) declares the reason why the Christian should glorify God amid persecution. Note that there are no lexical indicators for causality in this case. It is implied from context.

CASE: Case refers to the syntactical relationship of the substantive to other elements of a sentence. Although there is some disagreement among grammarians regarding the number of cases in a given language, the five major classes are nominative, accusative, dative, genitive, and vocative. Other grammarians also include ablative, locative, and instrumental. In many ancient languages, such as Latin or

Greek, nouns retain case endings that signify their grammatical case. However, case endings have fallen out of use in modern Romance languages (which are derivatives of Latin) and modern Greek. Likewise, English retains no remnants of an inflected case system, except among certain personal pronouns (e.g., nominative case "I," accusative and dative case "me," genitive case "mine"). Some Semitic languages, such as Akkadian and Ugaritic, also have case endings. However, except for some lingering vestiges, nouns in Biblical Hebrew have not retained any of their original case endings. See *Nominative case*; *Accusative case*; *Dative case*; *Genitive case*; *Vocative case*.

CLAUSE: A clause is the smallest grammatical unit consisting of one (and only one) subject and one (and only one) predicate. A clause may stand alone in a simple sentence (independent clause) or support other clauses within a compound sentence (dependent clause). See *Independent clause*; *Subordinate clause*.

COGNATE ACCUSATIVE: Cognate accusative is a syntactical structure in which the verb and its object are derived from the same root. In Hebrew, the tri-radical root system, along with its limited vocabulary, allows for the relative frequency of its use. In New Testament Greek, however, the cognate accusative is rare.

EXAMPLES:

1. In the second year of Nebuchadnezzar's reign, Nebuchadnezzar dreamed such dreams that his spirit was troubled and his sleep left him. (Dan 2:1)

   • The typical object for the verb "to dream" in the Hebrew Bible is the noun "dream." People were said to "dream dreams" rather than "have a dream." The noun "dream" is the cognate accusative of the verb "dreamed."

2.

חֵטְא חָטְאָה יְרוּשָׁלַם
עַל־כֵּן לְנִידָה הָיָתָה
כָּל־מְכַבְּדֶיהָ הִזִּילוּהָ
כִּי־רָאוּ עֶרְוָתָהּ

גַּם־הִיא נֶאֶנְחָה
וַתָּשָׁב אָחוֹר:

Jerusalem sinned grievously,
   so she has become a mockery;
all who honored her despise her,
   for they have seen her nakedness;
she herself groans,
   and turns her face away. (Lam 1:8)

- Both the verb "sinned" and the adverb "grievously" are derived from the same triradical root חטא, "sin." A more formal translation of the phrase "Jerusalem sinned grievously" (חָטְאָה חֵטְא יְרוּשָׁלַם) would be "Jerusalem sinned a sin."

3. ἀγωνίζου τὸν καλὸν ἀγῶνα τῆς πίστεως, ἐπιλαβοῦ τῆς αἰωνίου ζωῆς, εἰς ἣν ἐκλήθης καὶ ὡμολόγησας τὴν καλὴν ὁμολογίαν ἐνώπιον πολλῶν μαρτύρων.

Fight the good fight of the faith; take hold of the eternal life, to which you were called and for which you made [lit. "confessed"] the good confession in the presence of many witnesses. (1 Tim 6:12)

- This passage contains two cognate accusatives. The first is the noun "fight" (ἀγῶνα) following the imperative verb "fight" (ἀγωνίζου). The second is the noun "confession" (ὁμολογίαν) following the indicative verb "confess" (ὡμολόγησας), translated as "made" in the NRSV. Note that both cognate accusatives are in the accusative case, as would be expected.

COHORTATIVE: A cohortative is a verbal aspect in Biblical Hebrew that expresses wish or desire from the perspective of the speaker, that is, in the first person (either singular or plural). The cohortative only appears in the imperfect and is morphologically marked by the הָ- suffix. The hortatory subjunctive in Greek operates in a similar manner. See also *Hortatory subjunctive*; *Optative mood*; *Volitive*.

EXAMPLE:

1. וַיֹּאמֶר דָּוִיד אֶל־גָּד צַר־לִי מְאֹד אֶפְּלָה־נָּא בְיַד־יְהוָה כִּי־רַבִּים רַחֲמָיו מְאֹד וּבְיַד־אָדָם אַל־אֶפֹּל:

Then David said to Gad, "I am in great distress; let me fall into the hand of the LORD, for his mercy is very great; but let me not fall into human hands." (1 Chr 21:13)

- The verb "let me fall" (אֶפְּלָה־נָּא) is a first-person singular cohortative, indicating a wish or desire on the part of the speaker, David, and introducing the volitional clause, "let me fall into the hand of the LORD."

COLLECTIVE NOUN: A collective noun is one that represents an entire class. Usually, though not always, collective nouns are spelled as if they are singular and behave grammatically as singular nouns by taking a singular verbal conjugation. Exceptions are due to the fluidity and flexibility of rules among a language community.

EXAMPLES:

1. Then the whole assembly made a covenant with the king in the house of God. Jehoiada said to them, "Here is the king's son! Let him reign, as the LORD promised concerning the sons of David. (2 Chr 23:3)

- The word "assembly" is a collection of people gathered for a unified purpose. As a collective noun it takes the singular verbal conjugation.

2. הַהֵימִיר גּוֹי אֱלֹהִים וְהֵמָּה לֹא אֱלֹהִים
וְעַמִּי הֵמִיר כְּבוֹדוֹ בְּלוֹא יוֹעִיל:

Has a nation changed its gods,
    even though they are no gods?
But my people have changed their glory
    for something that does not profit. (Jer 2:11)

- Both "nation" (גּוֹי) and "people" (עַם) are collective nouns, representing the total population of a group. Each noun is governed by the third masculine singular Hiphil perfect verb "changed" (הֵמִיר).

3. καὶ πᾶς ὁ ὄχλος ἐζήτουν ἅπτεσθαι αὐτοῦ, ὅτι δύναμις παρ' αὐτοῦ ἐξήρχετο καὶ ἰᾶτο πάντας.

And all in the crowd were trying to touch him, for power came out from him and healed all of them. (Luke 6:19)

- In this particular case, the collective noun "the crowd" (ὁ ὄχλος) takes the third masculine plural verb "were trying" (ἐζήτουν), demonstrating that some collective nouns behave grammatically as plurals even though they are morphologically single.

COMPARATIVE: A comparative syntactical feature is one in which the relationship between two or more nouns is evaluated with respect to each other according to quality or quantity. English comparisons use words or phrases such as "more than," "greater than," or "less than." In Hebrew the most common means of expressing comparison is with the preposition מִן, although comparisons may be expressed in other ways. Most Greek adjectives take the comparative suffix -τερ- plus the appropriate case ending (e.g., νεός = new; νεώτερος = newer), while others require a change in vocabulary (e.g., ἀγαθός = good; κρείσσων = better).

EXAMPLES:

1. Two are better than one, because they have a good reward for their toil. (Eccl 4:9)

- According to this proverb in Ecclesiastes, two (people) have a greater qualitative value than one (person).

2.
הִרְבֵּית רֹכְלַיִךְ מִכּוֹכְבֵי הַשָּׁמָיִם
יֶלֶק פָּשַׁט וַיָּעֹף:

You increased your merchants
more than the stars of the heavens.
The locust sheds its skin and flies away. (Nah 3:16)

- The preposition מִן (with assimilated נ) is used in a comparative sense to signify the relationship between "your merchant
ships" (רֹכְלָיִךְ) and "the stars of the heavens" (כּוֹכְבֵי שָׁמַיִם).
The quantity of the former exceeds the quantity of the latter.

3. ὅτι τὸ μωρὸν τοῦ θεοῦ σοφώτερον τῶν ἀνθρώπων ἐστὶν καὶ τὸ
ἀσθενὲς τοῦ θεοῦ ἰσχυρότερον τῶν ἀνθρώπων.

For God's foolishness is wiser than human wisdom, and God's weakness
is stronger than human strength. (1 Cor 1:25)

- This passage contains two comparatives. In the first, "God's
foolishness" (τὸ μωρὸν τοῦ θεοῦ) surpasses the wisdom of
humanity. In the second, "God's weakness" (τὸ ἀσθενὲς τοῦ
θεοῦ) exceeds the strength of humanity. The -τερ- suffix
changes the adjective "wise" (σοφός) to the comparative "wiser
than" (σοφώτερον) and the adjective "strong" (ἰσχυρός) to the
comparative "stronger than" (ἰσχυρότερον).

COMPLEMENT: See *Object complement*; *Subject complement*.

COMMAND: See *Cohortative*; *Imperative mood*; *Jussive*.

CONCRETE NOUN: A concrete noun is a tangible person, place, or thing
that can be identified by one of the five senses.

EXAMPLES:

1. When anyone presents a grain offering to the LORD, the offering shall be of
choice flour; the worshiper shall pour oil on it, and put frankincense on it,
and bring it to Aaron's sons the priests. After taking from it a handful of
the choice flour and oil, with all its frankincense, the priest shall turn this
token portion into smoke on the altar, an offering by fire of pleasing odor
to the LORD. (Lev 2:1–2)

- Many, if not all, of the five senses can be used to experience the array of concrete nouns listed in this law concerning grain offerings.

2. וַיֹּאמֶר אֵלֶיהָ אֱלִישָׁע מָה אֶעֱשֶׂה־לָּךְ הַגִּידִי לִי מַה־יֶּשׁ־לְכִי בַּבָּיִת
וַתֹּאמֶר אֵין לְשִׁפְחָתְךָ כֹל בַּבַּיִת כִּי אִם־אָסוּךְ שָׁמֶן:

Elisha said to her, "What shall I do for you? Tell me, what do you have in the house?" She answered, "Your servant has nothing in the house, except a jar of oil." (2 Kgs 4:2)

- In this exchange between Elisha and a widow, four concrete nouns are mentioned: "house" (בַּיִת), "servant" (שִׁפְחָה), "jar" (אָסוּךְ), and "oil" (שָׁמֶן).

3. Ὑποπνεύσαντος δὲ νότου δόξαντες τῆς προθέσεως κεκρατηκέναι, ἄραντες ἆσσον παρελέγοντο τὴν Κρήτην.

When a moderate south wind began to blow, they thought they could achieve their purpose; so they weighed anchor and began to sail past Crete, close to the shore. (Acts 27:13)

- The noun "south wind" (νότου) is a concrete noun that can be indentified by touch (and possibly hearing and smell). Incidentally, "anchor" is not a concrete noun in the Greek as it is embedded in the meaning of the verb "weigh anchor" (ἄραντες).

CONDITIONAL SENTENCE: A conditional sentence provides the necessary situation to be met in order for a particular outcome to occur. The clause that provides the situation is known as the protasis. The clause that declares the outcome is known as the apodosis. Conditional sentences are typified by "if . . . then." Greek has four types of conditional sentences. First- and second-class conditions use εἰ with an indicative verb in the protasis. Third-class conditions use ἐάν followed by a subjunctive verb in the protasis. Fourth-class conditions use εἰ with the optative mood in the protasis. It should be noted that due to the decreased use of the optative mood in Hellenistic Greek, there are no complete fourth-class conditions in the New Testament. For the nuances of meaning on these conditional sentences, students should consult their Greek grammar textbook. See *Apodosis*; *Clause*; *Protasis*; *Subordinate clause*.

CONJUNCTION: A conjunction is a particle that links words, phrases, or clauses. There are three types of conjunctions. Coordinating conjunctions (e.g., and, or, yet) join two or more syntactical units. Correlative conjunctions work in equally weighted pairs (either . . . or; neither . . . nor; not only . . . but also). Subordinating conjunctions (e.g., although, because, since) join independent clauses with dependent clauses or introduce adverbial clauses. In both Hebrew and Greek many particles have the flexibility to function as any of the three types.

EXAMPLES:

1. They were archers, and could shoot arrows and sling stones with either the right hand or the left; they were Benjaminites, Saul's kindred. (1 Chr 12:2)

   • The correlative conjunction "either . . . or" joins the equally weighted pairs of "right hand" and "left."

2. וַאֲנִי יִסַּרְתִּי חִזַּקְתִּי זְרוֹעֹתָם וְאֵלַי יְחַשְּׁבוּ־רָע׃

   It was I who trained and strengthened their arms, yet they plot evil against me. (Hos 7:15)

   • The conjunction וְ functions as a coordinating conjunction, translated as "yet" in the NRSV, and connects two independent clauses.

3. Τεκνία, μηδεὶς πλανάτω ὑμᾶς· ὁ ποιῶν τὴν δικαιοσύνην δίκαιός ἐστιν, καθὼς ἐκεῖνος δίκαιός ἐστιν.

   Little children, let no one deceive you. Everyone who does what is right is righteous, just as he is righteous. (1 John 3:7)

   • The particle "just as" (καθώς) is a subordinating conjunction linking the dependent clause with the independent clause.

CONSTRUCT CHAIN: The construct chain is a distinctly Hebrew syntactic relationship in which two nouns are bound as a singular unit. The last noun in a construct chain is in the absolute state, while all others are in the construct state, whereby vowel reduction takes place where possible. English translations of the construct chain usually require "of" between the nouns within the chain. An example of a construct chain is "the day of the Lord." See *Genitive case*.

CONTRAST: A contrastive relationship is one in which a word, phrase, or clause is juxtaposed against another word, phrase, or clause, offering a correction to something in a previous clause. See *Disjunction*.

COORDINATING CONJUNCTION: See *Conjunction*.

COPULA: A copula is a verb of being (e.g., "is," "am") that equates the subject to the predicate. In verbless clauses the copula is implied.

1. In the beginning was the Word, and the Word was with God, and the Word was God. (John 1:1)

    • The final clause in the opening verse of John's Gospel equates "the Word" with "God" by using the copular verb "was."

2.
$$\text{יְהוָה אֲדֹנָי חֵילִי}$$
$$\text{וַיָּשֶׂם רַגְלַי כָּאַיָּלוֹת}$$
$$\text{וְעַל בָּמוֹתַי יַדְרִכֵנִי}$$

    God, the Lord, is my strength;
    > he makes my feet like the feet of a deer,
    > and makes me tread upon the heights. (Hab 3:19)

    • The Hebrew phrase translated as "God, the Lord, is my strength" (יְהוָה אֲדֹנָי חֵילִי) lacks a copula. As is common in Hebrew, especially poetry, the copula is assumed and can be supplied in translation.

3. καὶ αὐτὸς ἐπηρώτα αὐτούς, Ὑμεῖς δὲ τίνα με λέγετε εἶναι; ἀποκριθεὶς ὁ Πέτρος λέγει αὐτῷ, Σὺ εἶ ὁ Χριστός.

He asked them, "But who do you say that I am?" Peter answered him, "You are the Messiah." (Mark 8:29)

- Peter responds to Jesus's inquiry by stating that "you are the Messiah" (Σὺ εἶ ὁ Χριστός). By virtue of the copula, Jesus equals Messiah.

CORRELATIVE CONJUNCTION: See *Conjunction*.

— **D** —

DATIVE CASE: The dative case of a noun provides a reference for the action of a verb. Datives may be used to indicate an indirect object, location, means, time, agency, or association, among other uses. Ancient Semitic languages, including Hebrew, did not identify the dative as a case. However, nouns could function syntactically as a dative by virtue of their position within a sentence. Such dative-functioning nouns are typically preceded by a preposition, most frequently בְּ and לְ. Greek nouns in the dative case are indicated by their dative case endings, which vary depending on gender, number, and declension. See also *Case*.

EXAMPLES:

1. At the same time Tattenai the governor of the province Beyond the River and Shethar-bozenai and their associates came to them and spoke to them thus, "Who gave you a decree to build this house and to finish this structure?" (Ezra 5:3)

   - The second-person pronoun "you" is the indirect object of the verb "gave." Although English does not mark cases, "you" functions syntactically as a dative.

2. וְסָמַךְ אַהֲרֹן אֶת־שְׁתֵּי יָדָו עַל רֹאשׁ הַשָּׂעִיר הַחַי וְהִתְוַדָּה עָלָיו אֶת־כָּל־
עֲוֺנֹת בְּנֵי יִשְׂרָאֵל וְאֶת־כָּל־פִּשְׁעֵיהֶם לְכָל־חַטֹּאתָם וְנָתַן אֹתָם עַל־רֹאשׁ
הַשָּׂעִיר וְשִׁלַּח בְּיַד־אִישׁ עִתִּי הַמִּדְבָּרָה:

Then Aaron shall lay both his hands on the head of the live goat, and confess over it all the iniquities of the people of Israel, and all their transgressions, all their sins, putting them on the head of the goat, and sending it away into the wilderness <mark>by means of someone</mark> designated for the task. (Lev 16:21)

- The prepositional phrase "by means of someone" (בְּיַד־אִישׁ) functions as an instrumental dative, describing the means by which the "live goat" (הַשָּׂעִיר הַחַי) would be sent "into the wilderness" (הַמִּדְבָּרָה).

3. Καὶ <mark>τῇ ἡμέρᾳ</mark> τῇ τρίτη γάμος ἐγένετο ἐν <mark>Κανὰ</mark> τῆς Γαλιλαίας, καὶ ἦν ἡ μήτηρ τοῦ Ἰησοῦ ἐκεῖ.

On the third day there was a wedding in Cana of Galilee, and the mother of Jesus was there. (John 2:1)

- Due to the case endings in Koine Greek, it is relatively easy to identify the two dative nouns in this verse. The first dative noun "day" (τῇ ἡμέρᾳ) is a dative of time. The attributive adjective "third" (τῇ τρίτη) follows the rules of agreement and is likewise in the dative case. The second, "Cana" (Κανά), follows the preposition ἐν, which only takes the dative case.

DECLARATIVE SENTENCE: A declarative sentence is a syntactic unit composed of a subject and verb, contains a complete thought, and makes a statement of fact. Complex sentences may have layers of phrases and dependent clauses. Whereas the standard sentence structure in English is subject-verb-object, in Hebrew it is verb-subject-object. Due to its use of cases, Greek word order can afford to be much more fluid without losing the sense of a word's function within the sentence. See also *Clause*; *Phrase*; *Sentence*.

EXAMPLES:

1. So she went down to the threshing floor and did just as her mother-in-law had instructed her. (Ruth 3:6)

- This verse illustrates an example of a complex declarative sentence, where the subject, "she," has two predicates, "went down" and "did."

2. וַיַּךְ אֹתָם מֶלֶךְ בָּבֶל וַיְמִיתֵם בְּרִבְלָה בְּאֶרֶץ חֲמָת וַיִּגֶל יְהוּדָה מֵעַל אַדְמָתוֹ:

The king of Babylon struck them down and put them to death at Riblah in the land of Hamath. So Judah went into exile out of its land. (2 Kgs 25:21)

- This verse is composed of two sentences. The second sentence, "So Judah went into exile out of its land" (וַיִּגֶל יְהוּדָה מֵעַל אַדְמָתוֹ) is an example of a simple declarative sentence that follows the basic customary word order of a Hebrew sentence, where the two prepositional phrases occupy the usual spot of the direct object.

3. ὀφθαλμοὺς ἔχοντες μεστοὺς μοιχαλίδος καὶ ἀκαταπαύστους ἁμαρτίας, δελεάζοντες ψυχὰς ἀστηρίκτους, καρδίαν γεγυμνασμένην πλεονεξίας ἔχοντες, κατάρας τέκνα.

They have eyes full of adultery, insatiable for sin. They entice unsteady souls. They have hearts trained in greed. Accursed children! (2 Pet 2:14)

- The clause "they have hearts trained in greed" (καρδίαν γεγυμνασμένην πλεονεξίας ἔχοντες) is probably best understand as a simple declarative sentence, as translated by NRSV. Note that the sentence begins with the direct object "hearts" (καρδίαν) and concludes with the verb "they have" (ἔχοντες). Such a structure is not out of the ordinary in the Greek New Testament.

DEFINITENESS: Definiteness refers to the specificity of a noun. If it is a specific thing or group of things, it is said to be definite. If it could be any one thing among others, it is said to be indefinite. A noun is definite if it (1) has a definite article; (2) is associated with a possessive; (3) is modified by a demonstrative adjective; or (4) is a proper noun. However, in Greek the use of the article is very flexible, so rule (1) does not always apply in that language. When something is indefinite, it is translated into English with the indefinite article *a(n)*. Neither Hebrew nor Greek have a specific indicator for indefinite nouns.

Examples:

1. After these things King Ahasuerus promoted Haman son of Hammedatha the Agagite, and advanced him and set his seat above all the officials who were with him. (Esth 3:1)

    • All four types of a definite noun are present in this one verse. First, the definite article is present on both "the officials" and "the Agagite." Second, the possessive pronoun "his" identifies the owner of the "seat," indicating a particular seat. Third, the demonstrate adjective "these" specifies which "things" have happened in the narrative. Finally, there are two proper nouns, "Ahasuerus" and "Haman."

2. וָאֵרֶא וְהִנֵּה רוּחַ סְעָרָה בָּאָה מִן־הַצָּפוֹן עָנָן גָּדוֹל וְאֵשׁ מִתְלַקַּחַת וְנֹגַהּ
   לוֹ סָבִיב וּמִתּוֹכָהּ כְּעֵין הַחַשְׁמַל מִתּוֹךְ הָאֵשׁ:

    As I looked, a stormy wind came out of the north: a great cloud with brightness around it and fire flashing forth continually, and in the middle of the fire, something like gleaming amber. (Ezek 1:4)

    • Both "north" (הַצָּפוֹן) and the second use of "fire" (הָאֵשׁ) are definite by virtue of the fact that they are prefixed with the definite article "the" (הַ).

3. Δημητρίῳ μεμαρτύρηται ὑπὸ πάντων καὶ ὑπὸ αὐτῆς τῆς ἀληθείας· καὶ ἡμεῖς δὲ μαρτυροῦμεν, καὶ οἶδας ὅτι ἡ μαρτυρία ἡμῶν ἀληθής ἐστιν.

    Everyone has testified favorably about Demetrius, and so has the truth itself. We also testify for him, and you know that our testimony is true. (3 John 12)

- The three definite nouns in this verse are "Demetrius," "truth," and "testimony." "Demetrius" (Δημητρίῳ) is definite because it is a proper name, "the truth" (τῆς ἀληθείας) by virtue of the definite article, and "testimony" (ἡ μαρτυρία) due to the possessive pronoun "our" (ἡμῶν).

DEMONSTRATIVE ADJECTIVE: A demonstrative adjective is a modifying word that expressly states which noun among a potentially confusing set of nouns is being described. Demonstratives describing nouns that refer to something in close proximity are called "near" demonstratives (this, these), while demonstratives describing nouns that refer to something at a distance are called "far" demonstratives (that, those). Near demonstratives in Hebrew are זֶה, זֹאת, and אֵלֶּה. Far demonstratives in Hebrew are הוּא, הִיא, הֵמָּה/הֵם, and הֵנָּה/הֵן. Greek near demonstratives consist of all the declined forms of οὗτος, while far demonstratives consist of all the declined forms of ἐκεῖνος. Both Hebrew and Greek demonstrative adjectives follow the grammatical rules of regular adjectives. Furthermore, in Hebrew demonstrative adjectives are always definite. See *Attributive adjective.*

EXAMPLES:

1. Even on the male and female slaves, in those days, I will pour out my spirit. (Joel 2:29)

   - "Those" is a plural far demonstrative, modifying the plural noun "days."

2. וַיְהִי בַּשָּׁנָה הָרְבִיעִת לִיהוֹיָקִים בֶּן־יֹאשִׁיָּהוּ מֶלֶךְ יְהוּדָה הָיָה הַדָּבָר הַזֶּה אֶל־יִרְמְיָהוּ מֵאֵת יְהוָה לֵאמֹר:

   In the fourth year of King Jehoiakim son of Josiah of Judah, this word came to Jeremiah from the LORD (Jer 36:1)

   - "This" (הַזֶּה) is a near demonstrative, agreeing with "word" (הַדָּבָר) in gender (masculine), number (singular), and definiteness (definite).

3. καὶ τὰ νῦν λέγω ὑμῖν, ἀπόστητε ἀπὸ τῶν ἀνθρώπων τούτων καὶ ἄφετε αὐτούς· ὅτι ἐὰν ᾖ ἐξ ἀνθρώπων ἡ βουλὴ αὕτη ἢ τὸ ἔργον τοῦτο, καταλυθήσεται

So in the present case, I tell you, keep away from these men and let them alone; because if this plan or this undertaking is of human origin, it will fall. (Acts 5:38)

- This verse contains three near demonstrative adjectives. The first demonstrative, "these" (τούτων) is plural, while the twice-used demonstrative "this" (αὕτη; τοῦτο) is singular. Note that each demonstrative adjective agrees with the noun it modifies in case, gender, and number.

DEMONSTRATIVE PRONOUN: A demonstrative pronoun is a demonstrative adjective that acts as a substantive in a clause or sentence. As with demonstrative adjectives, demonstrative pronouns may be "near" (this, these) or "far" (that, those). The vocabulary for demonstrative pronouns is the same as the demonstrative adjectives in both Hebrew and Greek. Hebrew demonstrative pronouns are always anarthrous. See *Demonstrative adjective*; *Predicate adjective*.

EXAMPLES:

1. Let those curse it who curse the Sea, those who are skilled to rouse up Leviathan. (Job 3:8)

- The far demonstratives "those" function as the subject of their respective clauses. Therefore, they are called demonstrative pronouns in this context.

2. ‏אֵלֶּה תוֹלְדוֹת הַשָּׁמַיִם וְהָאָרֶץ בְּהִבָּרְאָם:

These are the generations of the heavens and the earth when they were created. (Gen 2:4)

- The near demonstrative pronoun "these" (‏אֵלֶּה) is the subject of the verbless clause "these are the generations" (‏אֵלֶּה תוֹלְדוֹת).

The demonstrative is indefinite and precedes the noun "generations" (תּוֹלְדוֹת), which is definite since it is in construct with the definite nouns "the heavens and the earth" (הַשָּׁמַיִם וְהָאָרֶץ).

3. καὶ λαβὼν ἄρτον εὐχαριστήσας ἔκλασεν καὶ ἔδωκεν αὐτοῖς λέγων, Τοῦτό ἐστιν τὸ σῶμά μου τὸ ὑπὲρ ὑμῶν διδόμενον· τοῦτο ποιεῖτε εἰς τὴν ἐμὴν ἀνάμνησιν.

Then he took a loaf of bread, and when he had given thanks, he broke it and gave it to them, saying, "This is my body, which is given for you. Do this in remembrance of me." (Luke 22:19)

- In both instances of the near demonstrative pronoun, "this" (τοῦτο) is in the nominative case and serves as the subject of its respective sentence.

DESIDERATIVE CLAUSE: A desiderative clause is one that expresses wish or desire. See *Volitive*.

DIRECT OBJECT: A direct object is a noun that receives the action of a transitive verb. Hebrew often signals the direct object with the so-called definite direct object marker אֶת/אֵת (sometimes called the sign of the accusative). In Greek the direct object normally takes the accusative case. See also *Accusative case*.

EXAMPLES:

1. As shoes for your feet put on whatever will make you ready to proclaim the gospel of peace. (Eph 6:15)

- The direct object of the transitive verb "proclaim" is "the gospel." It is the thing that is being proclaimed.

2. וַיֵּלֶךְ וַיִּקַּח אֶת־גֹּמֶר בַּת־דִּבְלָיִם וַתַּהַר וַתֵּלֶד־לוֹ בֵּן:

So he went and took Gomer daughter of Diblaim, and she conceived and bore him a son. (Hos 1:3)

- As a proper noun, "Gomer" (גֹּמֶר) is definite and, as the direct object of the transitive verb "took" (וַיִּקַּח), is preceded by the definite direct object marker אֶת־. The verb "she bore" (וַתַּהַר) is also transitive and has "son" (בֵּן) as its direct object.

3. τοίνυν ἐξερχώμεθα πρὸς αὐτὸν ἔξω τῆς παρεμβολῆς τὸν ὀνειδισμὸν αὐτοῦ φέροντες.

Let us then go to him outside the camp and bear the abuse he endured. (Heb 13:13)

- The direct object of the verb "bear" (φέροντες) is "the abuse" (τὸν ὀνειδισμόν), as indicated by the accusative case ending.

DISJUNCTION: Disjunction is a syntactical relationship in which two words, phrases, or clauses are contrasted with each other. English often uses a conjunction, such as "but" or "however," to demonstrate disjunction. In Hebrew the most common means of showing disjunction is by use of the disjunctive וְ, though other particles often carry a disjunctive meaning as well. Greek, like English, has numerous disjunctive particles that must be memorized as vocabulary items. See also *Conjunction*.

EXAMPLES:

1. A slack hand causes poverty,
   but the hand of the diligent makes rich. (Prov 10:4)

   - This proverb strikes a contrast between "a slack hand" and "the diligent," establishing a disjunctive relationship between the two types of people.

2.

אַשְׁרֵי־הָאִישׁ אֲשֶׁר
לֹא הָלַךְ בַּעֲצַת רְשָׁעִים
וּבְדֶרֶךְ חַטָּאִים לֹא עָמָד
וּבְמוֹשַׁב לֵצִים לֹא יָשָׁב׃
כִּי אִם בְּתוֹרַת יְהוָה חֶפְצוֹ
וּבְתוֹרָתוֹ יֶהְגֶּה יוֹמָם וָלָיְלָה׃

Happy are those
>who do not follow the advice of the wicked,
or take the path that sinners tread,
>or sit in the seat of scoffers;
but their delight is in the law of the Lᴏʀᴅ,
>and on his law they meditate day and night. (Ps 1:1–2)

- The opening verses of the Psalter present a contrast between
  the wise and the foolish, between the actions the wise
  person avoids and the actions the wise person takes. The
  Hebrew compound particle כִּי אִם ("but") is used to show the
  disjunction.

3. οὐ γὰρ ἔδωκεν ἡμῖν ὁ θεὸς πνεῦμα δειλίας ἀλλὰ δυνάμεως καὶ
ἀγάπης καὶ σωφρονισμοῦ.

For God did not give us a spirit of cowardice, but rather a spirit of power
and of love and of self-discipline. (2 Tim 1:7)

- The contrast between what God *has* given—"a spirit of power
  and of love and of self-discipline" (δυνάμεως καὶ ἀγάπης καὶ
  σωφρονισμοῦ)—and what God *has not* given—"a spirit of
  cowardice" (πνεῦμα δειλίας)—is made clear by the use of the
  strong disjunction "but rather" (ἀλλά).

—— E ——

ELLIPSIS: Ellipsis is the syntactical phenomenon in which certain elements of a phrase or clause are intentionally omitted but are apparent from context. In poetry especially ellipsis is sometimes referred to as "gapping."

Eₓₐₘₚₗₑₛ:

1. He subdued peoples under us,
>and nations under our feet. (Ps 47:3 [47:4 MT])

- Ellipsis takes place between lines one and two. The second line borrows its subject ("he") and predicate ("subdued") from the first.

2.

יֹאבַד יוֹם אִוָּלֶד בּוֹ
וְהַלַּיְלָה אָמַר הֹרָה גָבֶר:

Let the day perish in which I was born,
  and the night that said,
  "A man-child is conceived." (Job 3:3)

- The phrase "let perish" (יֹאבַד) is gapped in lines two and three, creating an ellipsis. Job expresses the desire that neither the day he was born nor the night he was conceived ever came into existence.

3. ἐπισκοποῦντες μή τις ὑστερῶν ἀπὸ τῆς χάριτος τοῦ θεοῦ, μή τις ῥίζα πικρίας ἄνω φύουσα ἐνοχλῇ καὶ δι' αὐτῆς μιανθῶσιν πολλοί, μή τις πόρνος ἢ βέβηλος ὡς Ἠσαῦ, ὃς ἀντὶ βρώσεως μιᾶς ἀπέδετο τὰ πρωτοτόκια ἑαυτοῦ.

See to it that no one fails to obtain the grace of God; that no root of bitterness springs up and causes trouble, and through it many become defiled. See to it that no one becomes like Esau, an immoral and godless person, who sold his birthright for a single meal. (Heb 12:15–16)

- The Greek participle translated as "see to it" (ἐπισκοποῦντες) carries the verbal idea throughout the three clauses. Although the participle only appears in the first clause, it is implied in the second and third clauses. The NRSV supplies it in translation prior to the third clause.

EPEXEGETICAL CLAUSE: An epexegetical word, phrase, or clause is one that stands in apposition to another word, phrase, or clause and provides clarification or specification to that which precedes it. English translations might introduce such a clause with "even," "namely," or "that is." In Hebrew and Greek an epexegetical clause is often introduced by a conjunction. See also *Apposition*; *Clause*; *Subordinate clause*.

EXAMPLES:

1. Only, you shall not eat flesh with its life, that is, its blood. (Gen 9:4)

   • The epexegetical phrase "its blood" specifies what constitutes the life force of flesh.

2. לִבְנֵי יוֹסֵף לִבְנֵי אֶפְרַיִם תּוֹלְדֹתָם לְמִשְׁפְּחֹתָם לְבֵית אֲבֹתָם בְּמִסְפַּר
   שֵׁמֹת מִבֶּן עֶשְׂרִים שָׁנָה וָמַעְלָה כֹּל יֹצֵא צָבָא׃

   The descendants of Joseph, namely, the descendants of Ephraim, their lineage, in their clans, by their ancestral houses, according to the number of names, from twenty years old and upward, everyone able to go to war. (Num 1:32)

   • Numbers 1:32–35 provides a census of Joseph's line. However, the author specifies which of Joseph's two sons receive the treatment, "namely, the descendants of Ephraim" (לִבְנֵי אֶפְרַיִם). In this case, no conjunction initiates the epexegetical clause.

3. Ἦν δὲ τὸ πάσχα καὶ τὰ ἄζυμα μετὰ δύο ἡμέρας. καὶ ἐζήτουν οἱ ἀρχιερεῖς καὶ οἱ γραμματεῖς πῶς αὐτὸν ἐν δόλῳ κρατήσαντες ἀποκτείνωσιν· ἔλεγον γάρ Μὴ ἐν τῇ ἑορτῇ, μήποτε ἔσται θόρυβος τοῦ λαοῦ.

   It was two days before the Passover and the festival of Unleavened Bread. The chief priests and the scribes were looking for a way to arrest Jesus by stealth and kill him; for they said, "Not during the festival, or there may be a riot among the people." (Mark 14:1–2)

   • During Old Testament times, "Passover" (τὸ πάσχα) and "the festival of Unleavened Bread" (τὰ ἄζυμα) were distinct festivals. By the time of the New Testament, though, these two festivals had become conflated (see Luke 22:1). Mark is likely not stating that it was two days before these two festivals but clarifying that the Passover also goes by the name "festival of Unleavened Bread." Although the NRSV translates the conjunction as "and," it is probably best to translate it here as "that is."

EXCLAMATORY SENTENCE: An exclamatory sentence is one that expresses strong feelings and is often introduced by an interjection. Exclamatory statements in English are frequently punctuated with the exclamation mark (!). See also *Interjection*.

EXAMPLES:

1. And I said: "Woe is me! I am lost, for I am a man of unclean lips, and I live among a people of unclean lips; yet my eyes have seen the King, the LORD of hosts!" (Isa 6:5)

   • In response to Isaiah's vision of God, he cried out in exclamation, "Woe is me!" The particle "woe" is an interjection that introduces the exclamatory statement and expresses the terror of the situation.

2. חָלִילָה לָּנוּ מִמֶּנּוּ לִמְרֹד בַּיהוָה וְלָשׁוּב הַיּוֹם מֵאַחֲרֵי יְהוָה לִבְנוֹת מִזְבֵּחַ לְעֹלָה לְמִנְחָה וּלְזָבַח מִלְּבַד מִזְבַּח יְהוָה אֱלֹהֵינוּ אֲשֶׁר לִפְנֵי מִשְׁכָּנוֹ:

   "Far be it from us that we should rebel against the LORD, and turn away this day from following the LORD by building an altar for burnt offering, grain offering, or sacrifice, other than the altar of the LORD our God that stands before his tabernacle!" (Josh 22:29)

   • Joshua expresses his distress over the potentiality of rebellion with the interjection, "Far be it" (חָלִילָה). One might also translate חָלִילָה as "May it never be!" The entire sentence introduced by the interjection is considered an exclamatory sentence.

3. Ἰδοὺ ἔρχεται μετὰ τῶν νεφελῶν,
   καὶ ὄψεται αὐτὸν πᾶς ὀφθαλμὸς
   καὶ οἵτινες αὐτὸν ἐξεκέντησαν,

καὶ κόψονται ἐπ' αὐτὸν πᾶσαι αἱ φυλαὶ τῆς γῆς.
ναί, ἀμήν.

Look! He is coming with the clouds;
    every eye will see him,
even those who pierced him;
    and on his account all the tribes of the earth will wail.
So it is to be. Amen. (Rev 1:7)

- John's first vision elicits surprise and amazement, expressed tersely with the interjection "look!" (Ἰδού), which stands alone as an exclamatory sentence.

— **F** —

FINITE VERB: A finite verb is a word that has a subject and performs the action of an independent clause. See also *Intransitive verb*; *Nonfinite verb*; *Transitive verb*.

EXAMPLES:

1. The time that Jehu reigned over Israel in Samaria was twenty-eight years. (2 Kgs 10:36)

   - The verb "reigned" is a finite verb.

2. וַיָּ֣מָת אִיּ֔וֹב זָקֵ֖ן וּשְׂבַ֥ע יָמִֽים׃

   And Job died, old and full of days. (Job 42:17)

   - The verb "died" (וַיָּמָת) is an example of a finite verb, performing the action of the independent clause.

3. πορευθέντες οὖν μαθητεύσατε πάντα τὰ ἔθνη, βαπτίζοντες αὐτοὺς εἰς τὸ ὄνομα τοῦ πατρὸς καὶ τοῦ υἱοῦ καὶ τοῦ ἁγίου πνεύματος, διδάσκοντες αὐτοὺς τηρεῖν πάντα ὅσα ἐνετειλάμην ὑμῖν· καὶ ἰδοὺ ἐγὼ μεθ' ὑμῶν εἰμι πάσας τὰς ἡμέρας ἕως τῆς συντελείας τοῦ αἰῶνος.

Go therefore and make disciples of all nations, baptizing them in the name of the Father and of the Son and of the Holy Spirit, and teaching them to obey everything that I have commanded you. And remember, I am with you always, to the end of the age. (Matt 28:19–20)

- The aorist imperative "make disciples" (μαθητεύσατε) is a finite verb and functions as the main verb in the Great Commission. Other finite verbs in this passage are "have commanded" (ἐνετειλάμην) and "am" (εἰμι).

FIRST PERSON: See *Number*; *Person*.

FUTURE TENSE: The future tense refers to events that have yet to take place or events that do not yet exist relative to a fixed moment in time. In Biblical Hebrew, the future tense is generally expressed by the imperfect, but it may also be expressed in other verbal forms, primarily the participle. Greek has a future-tense conjugation, but like Hebrew it can also express the future in other verbal forms, such as the participle. See also *Aspect*.

EXAMPLES:

1. I will surely make you least among the nations;
   you shall be utterly despised. (Obad 2)

   - As is common in the prophetic literature, the future tense is used to express what God will do to carry out his judgment. Here, the verbs "will make" and "shall be despised" are in the future tense.

2.

הִנֵּה אָנֹכִי שֹׁלֵחַ לָכֶם אֵת אֵלִיָּה הַנָּבִיא
לִפְנֵי בּוֹא יוֹם יְהוָה הַגָּדוֹל וְהַנּוֹרָא׃
וְהֵשִׁיב לֵב־אָבוֹת עַל־בָּנִים וְלֵב בָּנִים עַל־אֲבוֹתָם
פֶּן־אָבוֹא וְהִכֵּיתִי אֶת־הָאָרֶץ חֵרֶם׃

Lo, I will send you the prophet Elijah before the great and terrible day of the Lᴏʀᴅ comes. He will turn the hearts of parents to their children and the hearts of children to their parents, so that I will not come and strike the land with a curse. (Mal 4:5–6 [3:23–24 MT])

- The Old Testament concludes with these words promising a second Elijah. These verses employ three different verbal forms to express a future reality. First, the Lord "will send" (שֹׁלֵחַ), a participle preceded by an independent personal pronoun. This construction, especially when preceded by "lo" (הִנֵּה), is better rendered "I am about to send," but the notion of a future action is apparent in either case. Second, "will come" (אָבוֹא) is a Qal imperfect. Finally, the verbs "will turn" (וְהֵשִׁיב) and "will strike" (וְהִכֵּיתִי) are perfect consecutives, which receive their verbal aspect from the previous verbs, both of which are future in sense.

3. ὅτι αὐτὸς ὁ κύριος ἐν κελεύσματι, ἐν φωνῇ ἀρχαγγέλου καὶ ἐν σάλπιγγι θεοῦ, καταβήσεται ἀπ' οὐρανοῦ καὶ οἱ νεκροὶ ἐν Χριστῷ ἀναστήσονται πρῶτον

For the Lord himself, with a cry of command, with the archangel's call and with the sound of God's trumpet, will descend from heaven, and the dead in Christ will rise first. (1 Thess 4:16)

- Both "will descend" (καταβήσεται) and "will rise" (ἀναστήσονται) are future-tense verbs (marked by the σ augment), indicating that the events narrated have yet to occur.

—— G ——

GAPPING: See *Ellipsis*.

GENDER: Gender refers to the grammatical classification of a noun, whether it is feminine, masculine, or neuter. Nouns that are naturally gender specific tend to assume the same gender grammatically. However, as a grammatical category rather than a scientific category, some words do not follow the expected gender. In the biblical languages, gender is important for agreement among verbs, nouns, pronouns, and adjectives (and articles in Greek). In English, gender is assigned to the natural sex of the noun. Greek nouns may be masculine, feminine, or neuter, whereas Hebrew nouns may be masculine or feminine.

EXAMPLES:

1. So Boaz took Ruth and she became his wife. When they came together, the LORD made her conceive, and she bore a son. (Ruth 4:13)

   • According to the rules of English grammar, this verse has three masculine nouns and two feminine nouns. The three masculine nouns are "Boaz," "LORD," and "son." The three feminine nouns are "Ruth" and "wife."

2. לְבַעֲבוּר סַבֵּב אֶת־פְּנֵי הַדָּבָר עָשָׂה עַבְדְּךָ יוֹאָב אֶת־הַדָּבָר הַזֶּה וַאדֹנִי חָכָם כְּחָכְמַת מַלְאַךְ הָאֱלֹהִים לָדַעַת אֶת־כָּל־אֲשֶׁר בָּאָרֶץ׃

   In order to change the course of affairs your servant Joab did this. But my lord has wisdom like the wisdom of the angel of God to know all things that are on the earth. (2 Sam 14:20)

   • According to Hebrew grammar, 2 Samuel 14:20 has six masculine nouns and two feminine nouns. The masculine nouns are "affairs" (הַדָּבָר), "servant" (עֶבֶד), "Joab" (יוֹאָב), "lord" (אָדוֹן), "angel" (מַלְאַךְ), and "God" (הָאֱלֹהִים). The feminine nouns are "wisdom" (חָכְמָה) and "earth" (אֶרֶץ). Incidentally, the second instance of the masculine noun הַדָּבָר is left untranslated in the phrase "did this."

3. πέπεισμαι γὰρ ὅτι οὔτε θάνατος οὔτε ζωὴ οὔτε ἄγγελοι οὔτε ἀρχαὶ οὔτε ἐνεστῶτα οὔτε μέλλοντα οὔτε δυνάμεις οὔτε ὕψωμα οὔτε βάθος οὔτε τις κτίσις ἑτέρα δυνήσεται ἡμᾶς χωρίσαι ἀπὸ τῆς ἀγάπης τοῦ θεοῦ τῆς ἐν Χριστῷ Ἰησοῦ τῷ κυρίῳ ἡμῶν.

   For I am convinced that neither death, nor life, nor angels, nor rulers, nor things present, nor things to come, nor powers, nor height, nor depth, nor anything else in all creation, will be able to separate us from the love of God in Christ Jesus our Lord. (Rom 8:38–39)

- This passage contains a lengthy list of masculine, feminine, and neuter nouns. The masculine nouns are "death" (θάνατος), "angels" (ἄγγελοι), "God" (θεοῦ), "Christ" (Χριστῷ), "Jesus" (Ἰησοῦ), and "Lord" (κυρίῳ). The feminine nouns are "life" (ζωή), "rulers" (ἀρχαί), "creation" (κτίσις), and "love" (ἀγάπης). The neuter nouns include "powers" (δυνάμεις), "height" (ὕψωμα), and "depth" (βάθος).

GENITIVE ABSOLUTE: The genitive absolute is a grammatical construction found in the Greek language consisting of a participal in the genitive case together with either a noun or pronoun in the genitive case, forming a subordinate clause with respect to the main clause. See also: *Absolute phrase*; *Participle*; *Phrase*; *Subordinate clause*.

GENITIVE CASE: The genitive case establishes a relationship between two or more nouns, usually in a restrictive or descriptive sense. Some of the relationships include, but are not limited to, attribution, apposition, possession, objective, or subjective. In Semitic languages the genitive case was originally represented by the suffix -*i*(*m*), as seen in Akkadian and Ugaritic. Biblical Hebrew no longer marks its nouns with case endings, so the genitive case is typically expressed via the construct chain, in which the final word in the construct chain functions as a noun in the genitive case. Vestiges of the genitive case ending may linger in some nouns (e.g., עַל־דִּבְרָתִי ["according to the order of"] in Ps 110:4) and in certain particles containing the so-called *ḥireq compagnis* (connecting *ḥireq*), such as זוּלָתִי ("except") and בִּלְתִּי ("not"). In Greek, the genitive case may appear on nouns, pronouns, adjectives, and participles. Greek words in the genitive case are indicated by their genitive case endings, which vary depending on gender, number, and declension. See also *Case*; *Construct* (*chain*); *Objective genitive*; *Subjective genitive*.

Examples:

1. Who has directed the spirit of the Lord,
   > or as his counselor has instructed him? (Isa 40:13)

   - Although English does not mark its cases, here "of the Lord"
     functions as a genitive phrase, indicating possession of the
     spirit. The phrase "spirit of the Lord" could just as easily be
     translated as "the Lord's spirit."

2.

   הֲיְרֻצוּן בַּסֶּלַע סוּסִים
   אִם־יַחֲרוֹשׁ בַּבְּקָרִים
   כִּי־הֲפַכְתֶּם לְרֹאשׁ מִשְׁפָּט
   וּפְרִי צְדָקָה לְלַעֲנָה׃

   Do horses run on rocks?
   Does one plow the sea with oxen?
   But you have turned justice into poison
   and the fruit of righteousness into wormwood. (Amos 6:12)

   - The final word in the construct chain "the fruit of righteous-
     ness" (פְּרִי צְדָקָה) functions as a genitive of attribution. That
     is, "righteousness" (צְדָקָה) specifies the type of fruit that Israel
     has turned into wormwood.

3. τοῦτο γὰρ χάρις εἰ διὰ συνείδησιν θεοῦ ὑποφέρει τις λύπας
   πάσχων ἀδίκως.

   For it is a credit to you if, being aware of God, you endure pain while
   suffering unjustly. (1 Pet 2:19)

   - Since the noun "aware" (συνείδησιν) has a verbal idea, the
     corresponding genitive may be either subjective or objective.
     A subjective genitive performs the action of the verbal idea,
     while an objective genitive receives the action of the verbal idea.
     Here, "God" (θεοῦ) is not the one being made aware (subjec-
     tive) but is the one of whom others are being made aware, and
     thus the genitive construction is an objective genitive.

GERUND: A gerund is a verbal noun. In English, gerunds have the suffix *-ing* and may function as the subject of a finite verb (e.g., "*Walking* is good exercise"), the object of a verb (e.g., "She enjoys *walking*"), or the object of a preposition (e.g., "He gave up marathons for *walking*"). In biblical languages, the gerundive function is achieved via the active participle and the infinitive. See *Nonfinite verb*; *Participle*.

— **H** —

HENDIADYS: Hendiadys is the expression of a single thought through the connection of two or more words, usually joined by a conjunction.

EXAMPLES:

1. Know therefore that the Lᴏʀᴅ your God is God, the faithful God who maintains covenant loyalty with those who love him and keep his commandments, to a thousand generations, and who repays in their own person those who reject him. He does not delay but repays in their own person those who reject him. (Deut 7:9–10)

   • The Hebrew text behind the NRSV's "covenant loyalty" more literally reads "the covenant and the loyalty." These two words are so closely related both lexically and theologically that it is best to understand them functioning in hendiadys.

2. כִּי אָנֹכִי יָדַעְתִּי אֶת־הַמַּחֲשָׁבֹת אֲשֶׁר אָנֹכִי חֹשֵׁב עֲלֵיכֶם נְאֻם־יְהוָה מַחְשְׁבוֹת שָׁלוֹם וְלֹא לְרָעָה לָתֵת לָכֶם אַחֲרִית וְתִקְוָה׃

   For surely I know the plans I have for you, says the Lᴏʀᴅ, plans for your welfare and not for harm, to give you a future with hope. (Jer 29:11)

   • Many English translations treat "future and hope" (אַחֲרִית וְתִקְוָה) as two distinct ideas. However, the NRSV is probably correct to treat these closely related terms as representing a hendiadys, that is a "future with hope," which could also be understood as "a hopeful future."

3. ὅτι κατὰ δύναμιν, μαρτυρῶ, καὶ παρὰ δύναμιν, αὐθαίρετοι μετὰ
   πολλῆς παρακλήσεως δεόμενοι ἡμῶν τὴν χάριν καὶ τὴν κοινωνίαν
   τῆς διακονίας τῆς εἰς τοὺς ἁγίους

   For, as I can testify, they voluntarily gave according to their means, and
   even beyond their means, begging us earnestly for the privilege of sharing
   in this ministry to the saints. (2 Cor 8:3–4)

   • Rather than the Macedonian church begging for *both* "grace"
     (χάριν) *and* "fellowship" (κοινωνίαν), the idea expressed
     through hendiadys is captured by the NRSV as "the privilege
     of sharing" (τὴν χάριν καὶ τὴν κοινωνίαν).

HORTATORY SUBJUNCTIVE: A hortatory subjunctive is a verbal form
in Koine Greek in which a speaker exhorts his or her readers/hearers
to join him or her in an endeavor. The hortatory is always in the
subjunctive mood and is used in the first-person, usually in the plural.
The cohortative in Biblical Hebrew operates in a similar manner and
may be used in either the singular or plural. See also *Cohortative*;
Subjunctive mood; *Optative mood*; *Volitive*.

EXAMPLE:

1. Τοιγαροῦν καὶ ἡμεῖς τοσοῦτον ἔχοντες περικείμενον ἡμῖν νέφος
   μαρτύρων, ὄγκον ἀποθέμενοι πάντα καὶ τὴν εὐπερίστατον
   ἁμαρτίαν, δι' ὑπομονῆς τρέχωμεν τὸν προκείμενον ἡμῖν ἀγῶνα
   ἀφορῶντες εἰς τὸν τῆς πίστεως ἀρχηγὸν καὶ τελειωτὴν Ἰησοῦν,
   ὃς ἀντὶ τῆς προκειμένης αὐτῷ χαρᾶς ὑπέμεινεν σταυρὸν αἰσχύνης
   καταφρονήσας ἐν δεξιᾷ τε τοῦ θρόνου τοῦ θεοῦ κεκάθικεν.

   Therefore, since we are surrounded by so great a cloud of witnesses, let
   us also lay aside every weight and the sin that clings so closely, and let us
   run with perseverance the race that is set before us, looking to Jesus the
   pioneer and perfecter of our faith, who for the sake of the joy that was set
   before him endured the cross, disregarding its shame, and has taken his
   seat at the right hand of the throne of God. (Heb 12:1–2)

- The author of Hebrews is exhorting his audience to join with him in a lifelong pursuit of faithfulness, what he calls "the race that is set before us" (τὸν προκείμενον ἡμῖν ἀγῶνα). The exhortation, "let us run" (τρέχωμεν), is a first-person plural hortatory subjunctive.

—— I ——

IMPERATIVE MOOD: The imperative mood is the verbal form used to express a command. Technically speaking, it is a second-person volitive. Hebrew does not have mood as a grammatical category, but Hebrew imperatives are identifiable by their conjugation. Greek has four moods—indicative, imperative, optative, and subjunctive—each of which has distinct conjugations. See also *Imperative sentence*; *Mood*; *Volitive*.

EXAMPLES:

1. Comfort, O comfort my people,
   says your God. (Isa 40:1)

   - Due to the Babylonian exile, God commands the prophet to "comfort" his people Israel. The verb "comfort" is in the imperative mood.

2. תְּחִלַּת דִּבֶּר־יְהוָה בְּהוֹשֵׁעַ וַיֹּאמֶר יְהוָה אֶל־הוֹשֵׁעַ לֵךְ קַח־לְךָ אֵשֶׁת זְנוּנִים וְיַלְדֵי זְנוּנִים כִּי־זָנֹה תִזְנֶה הָאָרֶץ מֵאַחֲרֵי יְהוָה׃

   When the Lord first spoke through Hosea, the Lord said to Hosea, "Go, take for yourself a wife of whoredom and have children of whoredom, for the land commits great whoredom by forsaking the Lord." (Hos 1:2)

   - Following the historical heading in verse 1, the book of Hosea opens with a double imperative, "Go, take" (לֵךְ קַח), in which God instructs the prophet on what he must do.

3. βλέπετε μή τις ὑμᾶς ἔσται ὁ συλαγωγῶν διὰ τῆς φιλοσοφίας καὶ κενῆς ἀπάτης κατὰ τὴν παράδοσιν τῶν ἀνθρώπων, κατὰ τὰ στοιχεῖα τοῦ κόσμου καὶ οὐ κατὰ Χριστόν.

See to it that no one takes you captive through philosophy and empty deceit, according to human tradition, according to the elemental spirits of the universe, and not according to Christ. (Col 2:8)

- The apostle Paul exhorts the church in Colossae to "see to it" (βλέπετε) that they keep themselves on guard against external, non-Christocentric, influences. This is no mere wish on the apostle's part but an outright command. The verb βλέπετε is in the imperative mood.

IMPERATIVE SENTENCE: An imperative sentence is one in which the speaker issues a command to someone or something. Imperative sentences are governed by a verb or verbs in the imperative mood. See also *Imperative mood*; *Mood*; *Volitive*.

EXAMPLES:

1. Now if you are unwilling to serve the LORD, choose this day whom you will serve, whether the gods your ancestors served in the region beyond the River or the gods of the Amorites in whose land you are living; but as for me and my household, we will serve the LORD. (Josh 24:15)

   - Joshua issues a command to the Israelites to "choose," which is an imperative verb and introduces the imperative sentence that concludes with "in whose land you are living."

2. בֶּן־אָדָם הִנָּבֵא וְאָמַרְתָּ כֹּה אָמַר אֲדֹנָי יְהוִה הֵילִילוּ הָהּ לַיּוֹם:

   Mortal, prophesy, and say, Thus says the Lord GOD:
   Wail, "Alas for the day!" (Ezek 30:2)

   - The verbs "prophesy" (הִנָּבֵא) and "wail" (הֵילִילוּ) are both imperatives, the former being in the Niphal stem and the latter in the Hiphil. The following verb "and say" (וְאָמַרְתָּ)

is a perfect consecutive and carries the imperatival force of הָבָא, but it is not technically an imperative. The verse, then, consists of two imperative sentences.

3. ὁρᾶτε μή τις κακὸν ἀντὶ κακοῦ τινι ἀποδῷ, ἀλλὰ πάντοτε τὸ ἀγαθὸν διώκετε εἰς ἀλλήλους καὶ εἰς πάντας.

See that none of you repays evil for evil, but always seek to do good to one another and to all. (1 Thess 5:15)

- The imperative verbs "see" (ὁρᾶτε) and "seek" (διώκετε) are the first of ten imperatives within eight consecutive verses. This entire verse is an imperative sentence, comprised of two imperative clauses.

IMPERFECT TENSE: The imperfect tense is used to communicate an ongoing or continuous action, whether in the past, present, or the future with respect to the speaker. The imperfect is treated markedly different among English, Hebrew, and Greek. English grammars typically refer to the imperfect tense as the progressive tense of which there are six separate types: present progressive (e.g., "I am reading Hebrew"); past progressive (e.g., "I was reading Hebrew"); future progressive (e.g., "I will be reading Hebrew"); present perfect progressive (e.g., "I have been reading Hebrew"); past perfect progressive (e.g., "I had been reading Hebrew"); future perfect progressive (e.g., "I will have been reading Hebrew"). In both Hebrew and Greek the imperfect tense is a conjugated verbal form with features of the imperfective aspect. The imperfect tense in Hebrew generally expresses a present or future action, though context allows for more nuanced treatments. By contrast, the imperfect tense in Greek often relates to events in past time. Four major uses of the Greek imperfect include: (1) continuous action in the past; (2) habitual action in the past; (3) attempted action in the past; and (4) initiation of an action in the past. See also *Aspect*; *Imperfective aspect*; *Tense*.

EXAMPLES:

1. Hannah was praying silently; only her lips moved, but her voice was not heard; therefore Eli thought she was drunk. (1 Sam 1:13)

   • Hannah's prayer was a continuous action that took place in the past with respect to the narrator's perspective, so it is translated as an imperfect.

2.
   אֱלוֹהַ מִתֵּימָן יָבוֹא
   וְקָדוֹשׁ מֵהַר־פָּארָן סֶלָה
   כִּסָּה שָׁמַיִם הוֹדוֹ
   וּתְהִלָּתוֹ מָלְאָה הָאָרֶץ׃

   God comes from Teman,
   And the Holy One from Mount Paran. *Selah*.
   His splendor covers the heavens,
   And the earth is full of His praise. (Hab 3:3 NASB)

   • The verb "comes" (יָבוֹא) is in the imperfect tense and could be translated as a present or future. In this case context suggests that God's coming is a present and ongoing action rather than a future event. However, NRSV understands God's coming as a past event and translates יָבוֹא as "came."

3. Κἀκεῖθεν ἐξελθόντες παρεπορεύοντο διὰ τῆς Γαλιλαίας, καὶ οὐκ ἤθελεν ἵνα τις γνοῖ· ἐδίδασκεν γὰρ τοὺς μαθητὰς αὐτοῦ καὶ ἔλεγεν αὐτοῖς ὅτι ὁ υἱὸς τοῦ ἀνθρώπου παραδίδοται εἰς χεῖρας ἀνθρώπων, καὶ ἀποκτενοῦσιν αὐτόν, καὶ ἀποκτανθεὶς μετὰ τρεῖς ἡμέρας ἀναστήσεται.

   They went on from there and passed through Galilee. He did not want anyone to know it; for he was teaching his disciples, saying to them, "The Son of Man is to be betrayed into human hands, and they will kill him, and three days after being killed, he will rise again." (Mark 9:30–31)

   • The verbs "was teaching" (ἐδίδασκεν) and "saying" (ἔλεγεν) are both in the imperfect tense. The first imperfect verb expresses a continuous action in the past, while the second imperfect verb initiates an action in the past.

IMPERFECTIVE ASPECT: The imperfective aspect is a verbal quality that describes an action that is not yet complete. Verbs with an imperfective aspect in English are formed with a conjugation of "to be" followed by a present participle (e.g., "She is studying"). In Hebrew the imperfective aspect is manifest primarily through the imperfect tense or the participle. Greek imperfective aspect is communicated in a variety of ways including mood and tense. Students should consult their grammar textbooks for the precise ways in which aspect can be conveyed within each language. See *Aspect; Imperfect tense; Mood; Participle; Tense.*

INDEFINITE ARTICLE: See *Article; Definiteness.*

INDEPENDENT CLAUSE: An independent clause is one that contains a complete thought. It may be supported by subordinate clauses or stand on its own as a complete sentence. It is sometimes referred to as the main clause.

EXAMPLES:

1. So let us not grow weary in doing what is right, for we will reap at harvest time, if we do not give up. (Gal 6:9)

   - The sentence begins with the main clause, "So let us not grow weary in doing what is right." This clause could stand alone without the remainder of the sentence and still make complete sense.

2. וַיָּבֹאוּ עַד־גֹּרֶן נָכוֹן וַיִּשְׁלַח עֻזָּא אֶל־אֲרוֹן הָאֱלֹהִים וַיֹּאחֶז בּוֹ כִּי שָׁמְטוּ הַבָּקָר׃

   When they came to the threshing floor of Nacon, Uzzah reached out his hand to the ark of God and took hold of it, for the oxen shook it. (2 Sam 6:6)

   - The clause involving the actions of "Uzzah" (עֻזָּא) is the independent clause. If we removed the temporal and causal clause on either side of it, the clause could stand alone as its own sentence.

3. Ἀσπάζεταί σε τὰ τέκνα τῆς ἀδελφῆς σου τῆς ἐκλεκτῆς.

The children of your elect sister send their greetings. (2 John 13)

- This verse stands alone as a complete thought. In this case, the entire sentence is an independent clause.

INDEPENDENT PERSONAL PRONOUN: Independent personal pronouns are those words that take the place of the subject of a verb. Like English, both Hebrew and Greek have separate vocabulary words for independent personal pronouns. Personal pronouns in English are "I," "we," "you," "he," "she," "it," and "they." Students of biblical languages will need to learn the Hebrew and Greek personal pronouns as vocabulary items. See also *Antecedent*; *Pronoun*.

EXAMPLES:

1. He said, "Truly I tell you, this poor widow has put in more than all of them; for all of them have contributed out of their abundance, but she out of her poverty has put in all she had to live on." (Luke 21:3–4)

- In this teaching on giving, Jesus employs both the independent personal pronoun "I" and the independent personal pronoun "she," where "I" refers to Jesus and "she" refers to the widow from Luke 21:2.

2. וַיֹּאמֶר נָתָן אֶל־דָּוִד אַתָּה הָאִישׁ כֹּה־אָמַר יְהוָה אֱלֹהֵי יִשְׂרָאֵל אָנֹכִי מְשַׁחְתִּיךָ לְמֶלֶךְ עַל־יִשְׂרָאֵל וְאָנֹכִי הִצַּלְתִּיךָ מִיַּד שָׁאוּל:

Nathan said to David, "You are the man! Thus says the Lord, the God of Israel: I anointed you king over Israel, and I rescued you from the hand of Saul." (2 Sam 12:7)

- In Nathan's rebuke of David, the prophet uses both the independent personal pronoun "you" (אַתָּה) with reference to David and the independent personal pronoun "I" (אָנֹכִי) with reference to God.

3. κἀγὼ εἶπον, Κύριε, αὐτοὶ ἐπίστανται ὅτι ἐγὼ ἤμην φυλακίζων καὶ δέρων κατὰ τὰς συναγωγὰς τοὺς πιστεύοντας ἐπὶ σέ.

And I said, "Lord, they themselves know that in every synagogue I imprisoned and beat those who believed in you." (Acts 22:19)

- Here Paul uses three independent personal pronouns. "They" (αὐτοί) has the people of Jerusalem as its antecedent. "I" (ἐγώ) is in the nominative case and refers to Paul himself. "You" (σέ) is in the accusative case with reference to "Lord" (κύριε).

INDICATIVE MOOD: Verbs in the indicative mood express statements as fact, or otherwise express actions perceived to be real. Hebrew does not have mood as a grammatical category, but verbs may nonetheless be indicative based on their function. Greek has four moods—indicative, imperative, optative, and subjunctive—each of which has distinct conjugations. See also *Declarative sentence*; *Mood*.

EXAMPLES:

1. Therefore God gave them up in the lusts of their hearts to impurity, to the degrading of their bodies among themselves, because they exchanged the truth about God for a lie and worshiped and served the creature rather than the Creator, who is blessed forever! Amen. (Rom 1:24–25)

   - In these two verses we see four verbs in the indicative mood, each making a declarative statement about the condition of reality, first about God's actions, then about the actions of the godless.

2. וַיָּסַר הַמֶּלֶךְ אֶת־טַבַּעְתּוֹ מֵעַל יָדוֹ וַיִּתְּנָהּ לְהָמָן בֶּן־הַמְּדָתָא הָאֲגָגִי צֹרֵר הַיְּהוּדִים׃

   So the king took his signet ring from his hand and gave it to Haman son of Hammedatha the Agagite, the enemy of the Jews. (Esth 3:10)

   - Although Hebrew does not categorize mood, the two active verbs, "took" (lit. "removed"; וַיָּסַר) and "gave (it)" (וַיִּתְּנָהּ), make statements of fact and would be classified as indicative verbs.

3. Ἐπεφάνη γὰρ ἡ χάρις τοῦ θεοῦ σωτήριος πᾶσιν ἀνθρώποις.

   For the grace of God has appeared, bringing salvation to all. (Titus 2:11)

   - The verb "has appeared" (Ἐπεφάνη) is in the indicative mood, stating a fact regarding "the grace of God" (ἡ χάρις τοῦ θεοῦ).

INDIRECT OBJECT: An indirect object of a transitive verb is the recipient or benefactor of the direct object. Since an indirect object requires both a transitive verb and a direct object, indirect objects are uncommon. In Hebrew, indirect objects will be accompanied by a preposition, often לְ. In Greek, the indirect object will normally be in the dative case. See also *Dative case*; *Transitive verb*.

EXAMPLES:

1. Now these are the chiefs of David's warriors, who gave him strong support in his kingdom, together with all Israel, to make him king, according to the word of the LORD concerning Israel. (1 Chr 11:10)

   • The pronoun "him" serves as the indirect object of the transitive verb "gave." What the chief warriors gave was support. "David," the antecedent of "him," was the recipient of that support.

2. וַיֹּאמֶר יַעֲקֹב הִשָּׁבְעָה לִּי כַּיּוֹם וַיִּשָּׁבַע לוֹ וַיִּמְכֹּר אֶת־בְּכֹרָתוֹ לְיַעֲקֹב:

   Jacob said, "Swear to me first." So he swore to him, and sold his birthright to Jacob. (Gen 25:33)

   • The "birthright" (אֶת־בְּכֹרָתוֹ) is the thing Esau sold. The indirect object is "Jacob" (יַעֲקֹב), preceded by the preposition לְ. Put another way, Esau sold Jacob his birthright. Esau did not sell Jacob. Jacob was the beneficiary of the sale.

3. ἐκβαλὼν δὲ ἔξω πάντας ὁ Πέτρος καὶ θεὶς τὰ γόνατα προσηύξατο καὶ ἐπιστρέψας πρὸς τὸ σῶμα εἶπεν, Ταβιθά, ἀνάστηθι. ἡ δὲ ἤνοιξεν τοὺς ὀφθαλμοὺς αὐτῆς, καὶ ἰδοῦσα τὸν Πέτρον ἀνεκάθισεν. δοὺς δὲ αὐτῇ χεῖρα ἀνέστησεν αὐτήν· φωνήσας δὲ τοὺς ἁγίους καὶ τὰς χήρας παρέστησεν αὐτὴν ζῶσαν.

   Peter put all of them outside, and then he knelt down and prayed. He turned to the body and said, "Tabitha, get up." Then she opened her eyes, and seeing Peter, she sat up. He gave her his hand and helped her up. Then calling the saints and widows, he showed her to be alive. (Acts 9:40–41)

   • Peter "gave" (δοὺς) "his hand" (χεῖρα). Tabitha was the one who benefitted from Peter's gesture, thus the pronoun "her" (αὐτῇ) is the indirect object of the verb. Note that it is in the dative case.

INFINITIVE: An infinitive is a verbal noun that may function as a noun, adjective, or adverb. English infinitives are typically formed by adding the preposition "to" before a verb (e.g., "to stop"). The infinitive construct in Hebrew and the Greek infinitive may be used substantively, or it may be used adverbially to express purpose, result, or temporality. The Hebrew infinitive absolute most frequently adds emphasis to the finite verb, but it also has a broad range of uses. Students should consult their biblical-language grammars for the many nuanced ways in which an infinitive can function.

EXAMPLES:

1. Pray for us; we are sure that we have a clear conscience, desiring to act honorably in all things. (Heb 13:18)

   - The infinitive "to act" complements the participle "desiring," thus behaving as an adverbial infinitive of purpose.

2.
הִגִּיד לְךָ אָדָם מַה־טּוֹב
וּמָה־יְהוָה דּוֹרֵשׁ מִמְּךָ
כִּי אִם־עֲשׂוֹת מִשְׁפָּט וְאַהֲבַת חֶסֶד
וְהַצְנֵעַ לֶכֶת עִם־אֱלֹהֶיךָ׃

   He has told you, O mortal, what is good;
   and what does the Lord require of you
   but to do justice, and to love kindness,
   and to walk humbly with your God? (Micah 6:8)

   - This well-known passage contains both types of Hebrew infinitives. The infinitive construct is used twice, "to do" (עֲשׂוֹת) and "to walk" (לֶכֶת), as substantival infinitives. "Humbly" (הַצְנֵעַ) is a Hiphil infinitive absolute, functioning adverbially by modifying how one should walk with God.

3. Ἐμοὶ γὰρ τὸ ζῆν Χριστὸς καὶ τὸ ἀποθανεῖν κέρδος.

   For to me, living is Christ and dying is gain. (Phil 1:21)

- The two infinitives in this passage, "living" (ζῆν) and "dying" (ἀποθανεῖν) are used substantively as predicate nominatives.

INTENSIVE PRONOUN: An intensive pronoun is one that adds emphasis to the subject. English examples of the intensive pronoun are "myself," "yourself," "himself," "herself," "itself," "ourselves," "yourselves," and "themselves." In Hebrew and Greek, the use of an independent personal pronoun as the subject of the verb is often used for emphasis and can be translated as an intensive pronoun. In Greek, anarthrous αὐτός can be used in all three persons as an intensive pronoun. See also *Pronoun.*

EXAMPLES:

1. I myself will show him how much he must suffer for the sake of my name. (Acts 9:16)

   - The subject of the verb is emphasized by its reduplication via the intensive personal pronoun "myself." The speaker (Jesus) wishes to make emphatic that he is the one who must suffer, and not another.

2. יְהוָה אֱלֹהֶיךָ הוּא עֹבֵר לְפָנֶיךָ הוּא־יַשְׁמִיד אֶת־הַגּוֹיִם הָאֵלֶּה מִלְּפָנֶיךָ וִירִשְׁתָּם יְהוֹשֻׁעַ הוּא עֹבֵר לְפָנֶיךָ כַּאֲשֶׁר דִּבֶּר יְהוָה:

   The LORD your God himself will cross over before you. He will destroy these nations before you, and you shall dispossess them. Joshua also will cross over before you, as the LORD promised. (Deut 31:3)

   - Moses wants the Israelites to be sure that it is "the LORD your God" (יְהוָה אֱלֹהֶיךָ) and no one else who will cross the Jordan ahead of them, so he adds the intensive pronoun "himself" (הוּא).

3. πῶς δύνασαι λέγειν τῷ ἀδελφῷ σου, Ἀδελφέ, ἄφες ἐκβάλω τὸ κάρφος τὸ ἐν τῷ ὀφθαλμῷ σου, αὐτὸς τὴν ἐν τῷ ὀφθαλμῷ σου δοκὸν οὐ βλέπων; ὑποκριτά, ἔκβαλε πρῶτον τὴν δοκὸν ἐκ τοῦ ὀφθαλμοῦ σου, καὶ τότε διαβλέψεις τὸ κάρφος τὸ ἐν τῷ ὀφθαλμῷ τοῦ ἀδελφοῦ σου ἐκβαλεῖν.

Or how can you say to your neighbor, "Friend, let me take out the speck in your eye," when you **yourself** do not see the log in your own eye? You hypocrite, first take the log out of your own eye, and then you will see clearly to take the speck out of your neighbor's eye." (Luke 6:42)

- Jesus uses the intensive pronoun "yourself" (αὐτός) to emphasize the hypocrisy of failing to see fault in oneself before finding fault in others.

INTERJECTION: An interjection is a word or particle that expresses emotion. Examples of interjections in English are "ah," "hey," and "wow." Examples in Hebrew include, but are not limited to, אָח ("ah!"), הוֹי ("woe!"), הֵנֵּה/הֶן ("look!"), and חָלִילָה ("far be it!"). Greek has at least eight interjections: ἄγε ("come!"), δεῦρο ("come!"), δεῦτε ("come!"), ἔα ("hey!"), ἴδε ("look!"), ἰδού ("look!"), οὐαί ("woe!"), and ὦ ("O!"). See also *Exclamatory sentence*.

Examples:

1. Ah, you that turn justice to wormwood,
    and bring righteousness to the ground! (Amos 5:7)

- The interjection "ah" is employed to convey contempt against those who commit injustices.

2.
הֶן־עָם כְּלָבִיא יָקוּם
וְכַאֲרִי יִתְנַשָּׂא
לֹא יִשְׁכַּב עַד־יֹאכַל טֶרֶף
וְדַם־חֲלָלִים יִשְׁתֶּה׃

Look, a people rising up like a lioness,
    and rousing itself like a lion!
It does not lie down until it has eaten the prey
    and drunk the blood of the slain. (Num 23:24)

- "Look" (הֶן) is an interjection expressing surprise in how "the people" (עָם) Israel will defeat Balak, not vice versa.

3. οὐαὶ αὐτοῖς, ὅτι τῇ ὁδῷ τοῦ Κάϊν ἐπορεύθησαν καὶ τῇ πλάνῃ τοῦ Βαλαὰμ μισθοῦ ἐξεχύθησαν καὶ τῇ ἀντιλογίᾳ τοῦ Κόρε ἀπώλοντο.

Woe to them! For they go the way of Cain, and abandon themselves to Balaam's error for the sake of gain, and perish in Korah's rebellion. (Jude 11)

- "Woe" (οὐαί) is an interjection used to communicate a distressed attitude toward false teachers.

INTERROGATIVE PRONOUN: An interrogative word that introduces a question. The English interrogative pronouns are "what," "which," "who," "whom," and "whose." The two main interrogative pronouns in Hebrew are מִי ("who?") and מָה ("what?"). The Greek interrogative pronouns are declined from τίς ("who?" "whom?" "whose?" "what?"). See *Interrogative sentence*.

INTERROGATIVE SENTENCE: An interrogative is a statement, usually introduced by an interrogative pronoun, that poses a question and expects a response. In English interrogative sentences are generally followed by a question mark. Hebrew interrogatives are often preceded by the interrogative -הֲ (-הַ, -הֶ) or an interrogative pronoun. Modern versions of the Greek New Testament signify interrogative statements with a semicolon (;). See also *Interrogative pronoun*.

EXAMPLES:

1. So the king said to me, "Why is your face sad, since you are not sick? This can only be sadness of the heart." Then I was very much afraid. (Neh 2:2)

- Nehemiah was visibly unsettled by the news of Jerusalem's walls, which prompted King Artaxerxes to inquire about his disposition. The statement, "Why is your face sad, since you are not sick?" is stated as an interrogative, posing a question to be answered. "Why" is an interrogative pronoun.

2.

וַיַּעַן־יְהוָה אֶת־אִיּוֹב מִן הַסְּעָרָה וַיֹּאמַר:
מִי זֶה מַחְשִׁיךְ עֵצָה בְמִלִּין בְּלִי־דָעַת:

Then the Lᴏʀᴅ answered Job out of the whirlwind:

"Who is this that darkens counsel by words without knowledge?"
(Job 38:1–2)

- When the Lᴏʀᴅ responds to Job's chapters-long plea for a hearing before his divine vindicator, the Lᴏʀᴅ replies with the interrogative statement, "Who is this that darkens counsel by words without knowledge?" (מִי זֶה מַחְשִׁיךְ עֵצָה בְמִלִּין בְּלִי־דָעַת) introduced by the interrogative pronoun "who"(מִי).

3. Ὦ ἀνόητοι Γαλάται, τίς ὑμᾶς ἐβάσκανεν, οἷς κατ' ὀφθαλμοὺς Ἰησοῦς Χριστὸς προεγράφη ἐσταυρωμένος;

You foolish Galatians! Who has bewitched you? It was before your eyes that Jesus Christ was publicly exhibited as crucified! (Gal 3:1)

- Paul poses this question to the Galatians: "Who has bewitched you?" (τίς ὑμᾶς ἐβάσκανεν). The interrogative statement is introduced by the interrogative pronoun "who" (τίς). Note that the question mark (;) is placed at the conclusion of the verse rather than immediately after the interrogative statement.

INTRANSITIVE VERB: An intransitive verb is one that describes an action and does not take a direct object. Some verbs are somewhat fluid in that they can take a direct object in some cases (e.g., "Jill ran the sail up the mast"), but do not require one (e.g., "Jill ran to school"). See also *Direct object*; *Transitive verb*.

Exᴀᴍᴘʟᴇs:

1. Then David slept with his ancestors, and was buried in the city of David. (1 Kgs 2:10)

- The verb "slept" is intransitive. It expresses an action but cannot take a direct object. By contrast, "buried" is a transitive verb that, if not for the fact that it is in the passive voice, could take a direct object.

2. וַיִּקְרַע יְהוֹשֻׁעַ שִׂמְלֹתָיו וַיִּפֹּל עַל־פָּנָיו אַרְצָה לִפְנֵי אֲרוֹן יְהוָה עַד־הָעֶרֶב
הוּא וְזִקְנֵי יִשְׂרָאֵל וַיַּעֲלוּ עָפָר עַל־רֹאשָׁם:

Then Joshua tore his clothes, and fell to the ground on his face before the
ark of the Lᴏʀᴅ until the evening, he and the elders of Israel; and they put
dust on their heads. (Josh 7:6)

- When used in reference to the subject, the verb "fell" (וַיִּפֹּל) is
  an intransitive verb because it cannot take a direct object. Of
  course, when referring to the action of cutting down a tree,
  "to fell" can be a transitive verb, where "tree" would be the
  direct object (see, e.g., 2 Kgs 3:25).

3. καὶ ἦν ἡμέρας τρεῖς μὴ βλέπων καὶ οὐκ ἔφαγεν οὐδὲ ἔπιεν.

For three days he was without sight, and neither ate nor drank. (Acts 9:9)

- Both "ate" (ἔφαγεν) and "drank" (ἔπιεν) can take direct
  objects. One can eat bread and drink wine, for example. However, neither verb requires a direct object as in this example,
  thus qualifying them as intransitive verbs.

INSTRUMENTAL CASE: The instrumental case expresses the means
by which or with which the verb acts upon the substantive. Most
grammarians view the instrumental case as a subset of the dative
case. In Greek, substantives of instrument often carry the dative case
ending. See *Case*; *Dative case*.

— J —

JUSSIVE: A jussive is a verbal aspect in Biblical Hebrew that expresses
wish or desire, normally in the third person, but occasionally in the
second person. See also *Optative mood*; *Volitive*.

Eχᴀᴍᴘʟᴇ:

1. הַכֹּל נָתַן אֲרַוְנָה הַמֶּלֶךְ לַמֶּלֶךְ וַיֹּאמֶר אֲרַוְנָה אֶל־הַמֶּלֶךְ יְהוָה אֱלֹהֶיךָ
יִרְצֶךָ:

"All this, O king, Araunah gives to the king." And Araunah said to the king, "May the Lᴏʀᴅ your God respond favorably to you." (2 Sam 24:23)

- The verb "may respond favorably to you" (יִרְצֶךָ) is a third masculine singular jussive form that expresses the wish on the part of "Araunah" (אֲרַוְנָה) for "the Lᴏʀᴅ your God" (יְהוָה אֱלֹהֶיךָ) to work in the king's interest.

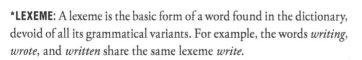

*LEXEME: A lexeme is the basic form of a word found in the dictionary, devoid of all its grammatical variants. For example, the words *writing*, *wrote*, and *written* share the same lexeme *write*.

*LINGUISTICS: Linguistics pertains to the formal study of language and its structure, including morphology, phonetics, semantics, and syntax.

LINKING VERB: A linking verb is used to establish a relationship between the subject of a clause and an adjective, another noun, or a verbal noun (e.g., a participle) that describes the subject. A linking verb is either a verb of being or a verb that can be replaced by a verb of being (e.g., "appeared," "seemed") and still make sense. See also *Copula*.

Exᴀᴍᴘʟᴇs:

1. Days are coming when all that is in your house, and that which your ancestors have stored up until this day, shall be carried to Babylon; nothing shall be left, says the Lᴏʀᴅ. (2 Kgs 20:17//Isa 39:6)

   - The verb "are" links the noun "days" with the participle "coming." In the Hebrew, the verb is absent from the text.

2. אִישׁ הָיָה בְאֶרֶץ־עוּץ אִיּוֹב שְׁמוֹ וְהָיָה הָאִישׁ הַהוּא תָּם וְיָשָׁר וִירֵא אֱלֹהִים וְסָר מֵרָע׃

> There was once a man in the land of Uz whose name was Job. That man was blameless and upright, one who feared God and turned away from evil. (Job 1:1)

- The verb "was" (הָיָה) links the noun "man" (אִישׁ) with the prepositional phrase "in the land of Uz" (בְאֶרֶץ־עוּץ). The phrase אִישׁ הָיָה בְאֶרֶץ־עוּץ could just as easily be translated, "A man was in the land of Uz," more clearly demonstrating the linking function of the verb הָיָה.

3. Ἐγώ εἰμι τὸ Ἄλφα καὶ τὸ Ὦ, λέγει κύριος ὁ θεός, ὁ ὢν καὶ ὁ ἦν καὶ ὁ ἐρχόμενος, ὁ παντοκράτωρ.

> "I am the Alpha and the Omega," says the Lord God, who is and who was and who is to come, the Almighty. (Rev 1:8)

- The verb "am" (εἰμί) links the speaker, "I" (ἐγώ), with "the Alpha" (τὸ Ἄλφα) and "the Omega" (τὸ Ὦ).

LOCATIVE CASE: The locative case is used to express the relative position of a substantive. Most grammarians view the locative case as a subset of the dative case. In Greek, substantives of location carry the dative case ending. See *Case*; *Dative case*.

— **M** —

MAIN CLAUSE: See *Independent clause*.

MIDDLE VOICE: The middle voice is used in Greek to express the idea that the subject of the verb is also in some way the object of the verb or otherwise participates in and/or benefits from the action. In the middle voice the subject receives greater focus. English translations of the middle voice often require the addition of a reflexive pronoun such as "himself" or "herself," except in certain situations where the subject of the verb inherently acts upon itself by virtue of the character of the verb (e.g., "take," "remember"). Hebrew can express the middle voice via the passive verbal forms Hophal, Hithpael, Niphal, and Pual. See also *Reflexive pronoun*; *Reflexive verb*.

EXAMPLES:

1. Throwing down the pieces of silver in the temple, he departed; and he went and hanged himself. (Matt 27:5)

   • Judas was both the one doing the hanging and the one being hanged; thus the verb is represented by the middle voice (as is clear from the Greek text). Note the use of the reflexive pronoun "himself" to convey the middle voice into English.

2. וַיַּעֲלוּ כָל־הָעָם אַחֲרָיו וְהָעָם מְחַלְּלִים בַּחֲלִלִים וּשְׂמֵחִים שִׂמְחָה גְדוֹלָה וַתִּבָּקַע הָאָרֶץ בְּקוֹלָם׃

   And all the people went up following him, playing on pipes and rejoicing with great joy, so that the earth quaked at their noise. (1 Kgs 1:40)

   • Since the verb "quaked" (וַתִּבָּקַע) is in the Niphal verbal stem but has an active sense to it, one could translate the verb as "quaked itself." Yet by virtue of the definition of "quake," such a translation would be redundant. This is an example of the middle voice in Hebrew.

3. ἡμέρας παρατηρεῖσθε καὶ μῆνας καὶ καιροὺς καὶ ἐνιαυτούς,

   You are observing special days, and months, and seasons, and years. (Gal 4:10)

   • The verb "are observing" (παρατηρεῖσθε) is marked morphologically as a middle-voice verb. Moreover, the action of observing is one that has direct impact on the subject.

MODIFIER: A modifier is a word, phrase, or clause that provides a clarifying attribute to another word, phrase, or clause. All adjectives are modifiers, but not all modifiers are adjectives. See also *Adjective*.

EXAMPLES:

1. Upon my bed at night
       I sought him whom my soul loves;
   I sought him, but found him not;
       I called him, but he gave no answer. (Song 3:1)

- The phrase "whom my soul loves" is a relative clause modifying "him," elucidating precisely whom the lover sought.

2.   וָאָשׁוּב וָאֶשָּׂא עֵינַי וָאֶרְאֶה וְהִנֵּה מְגִלָּה עָפָה׃

Again I looked up and saw a flying scroll. (Zech 5:1)

- The word "flying" (עָפָה) clarifies what type of "scroll" (מְגִלָּה) the prophet saw. Although עָפָה behaves like an adjective, it is actually a feminine singular participle.

3. Ἰούδας Ἰησοῦ Χριστοῦ δοῦλος, ἀδελφὸς δὲ Ἰακώβου, τοῖς ἐν θεῷ πατρὶ ἠγαπημένοις καὶ Ἰησοῦ Χριστῷ τετηρημένοις κλητοῖς.

Jude, a servant of Jesus Christ and brother of James,

To those who are called, who are beloved in God the Father and kept safe for Jesus Christ. (Jude 1)

- The audience of Jude's letter is "those who are called" (τοῖς . . . κλητοῖς). To ensure that his audience is clear on what that means, Jude inserts the modifying clause "who are beloved in God the Father and kept safe for Jesus Christ" (ἐν θεῷ πατρὶ ἠγαπημένοις καὶ Ἰησοῦ Χριστῷ τετηρημένοις).

MOOD: Mood is a verbal category used to describe how a verb operates in a sentence, whether as a command (imperative), statement of fact (indicative), question (interrogative), wish (optative), or potential (subjunctive). See *Imperative mood*; *Indicative mood*; *Optative mood*; *Subjunctive mood*.

*MORPHEME: A morpheme is the simplest grammatical unit in a language. For example, the word *unwittingly* is comprised of three morphemes: the prefix /un/, the adjective /witting/, and the adverbial suffix /ly/.

*MORPHOLOGY: Morphology pertains to the structure of words, paying special attention to the parts (morphemes) that comprise words. See also *Morpheme*.

— **N** —

NOMINATIVE: A nominative is a word that functions as the subject of a clause. See *Nominative case*; *Noun*.

NOMINATIVE CASE: The nominative case is the one assumed by the subject of a clause. As with the entire case system, English grammar does not indicate the nominative case, except in personal pronouns. Moreover, grammarians of the English language refer to nouns in the nominative position as the subject of the independent clause. Greek nouns in the nominative case are indicated by their nominative case endings, which vary depending on gender, number, and declension. In Semitic languages the nominative case was originally represented by the -*u*(*m*) suffix, as seen in Akkadian and Ugaritic. Biblical Hebrew, a Semitic language coming at a later stage of development, no longer marked its nouns with case endings. However, some proper names have retained their nominative case ending by virtue of the morpheme /וּ/ (e.g., גַּשְׁמוּ in Neh 6:6).

EXAMPLES:

1. When it was noon, darkness came over the whole land until three in the afternoon. (Mark 15:33)

   • The noun "darkness" is the subject of the sentence and is in the nominative position.

2. וַיִּסְעוּ בְּנֵי יִשְׂרָאֵל וַיַּחֲנוּ בְּעַרְבוֹת מוֹאָב מֵעֵבֶר לְיַרְדֵּן יְרֵחוֹ׃

   The Israelites set out, and camped in the plains of Moab across the Jordan from Jericho. (Num 22:1)

   • Since Hebrew has lost its original case endings (with rare exception), there are virtually no morphologically tagged words in the nominative case. Nonetheless, "the Israelites" (בְּנֵי יִשְׂרָאֵל) serves as the subject of the sentence and is therefore considered to be in the nominative case, even if it is not marked as such.

3. Ἡ χάρις τοῦ κυρίου Ἰησοῦ Χριστοῦ καὶ ἡ ἀγάπη τοῦ θεοῦ καὶ ἡ κοινωνία τοῦ ἁγίου πνεύματος μετὰ πάντων ὑμῶν.

The grace of the Lord Jesus Christ, the love of God, and the communion of the Holy Spirit be with all of you. (2 Cor 13:13)

- Paul's conclusion to this letter to Corinth includes three nouns in the nominative case. These three nouns—"the grace" (ἡ χάρις), "the love" (ἡ ἀγάπη), and "the communion" (ἡ κοινωνία)—function as the subjects of the sentence. All three nouns are in the nominative case.

NONFINITE VERB: A nonfinite verb is one that is incapable of performing the main action of an independent clause and does not show person or number. Furthermore, in English and Hebrew, nonfinite verbs do not have tense. Examples of nonfinite verbs are infinitives, participles, and gerunds. See also *Finite verb; Infinitive; Gerund; Participle*.

Examples:

1. I am going to lay a fleece of wool on the threshing floor; if there is dew on the fleece alone, and it is dry on all the ground, then I shall know that you will deliver Israel by my hand, as you have said. (Judg 6:37)

- The infinitive "to lay" is an example of a nonfinite verb.

2. וַיְהִי כַּאֲשֶׁר־תַּמּוּ כָל־הַגּוֹי לְהִמּוֹל וַיֵּשְׁבוּ תַחְתָּם בַּמַּחֲנֶה עַד חֲיוֹתָם׃

When the circumcising of all the nation was done, they remained in their places in the camp until they were healed. (Josh 5:8)

- The phrase "the circumcising" (לְהִמּוֹל) is a nonfinite verb both in the Hebrew, where it is an infinitive, and in the English translation, where it is a gerund.

3. καὶ πᾶν ὅ τι ἐὰν ποιῆτε ἐν λόγῳ ἢ ἐν ἔργῳ, πάντα ἐν ὀνόματι κυρίου Ἰησοῦ, εὐχαριστοῦντες τῷ θεῷ πατρὶ δι᾿ αὐτοῦ.

And whatever you do, in word or deed, do everything in the name of the Lord Jesus, giving thanks to God the Father through him. (Col 3:17)

- The participle "giving thanks" (εὐχαριστοῦντες) introduces a subordinate clause, so it cannot perform the action of the sentence. It is an example of a nonfinite verb.

NONRESTRICTIVE CLAUSE: See *Relative clause.*

NOUN: A noun is a word that indicates a person, place, thing, or idea. See also *Abstract noun; Concrete noun; Proper noun.*

EXAMPLES:

1. Three things are too wonderful for me;
   four I do not understand:
   the way of an eagle in the sky,
   the way of a snake on a rock,
   the way of a ship on the high seas,
   and the way of a man with a girl. (Prov 30:18–19)

   - This proverb lists ten separate nouns. Two are people ("man," "girl"), three are places ("sky," "rock," "seas"), four are things ("things," "eagle," "snake," "ship") and one is an idea ("way").

2.

וַיִּגַּל כַּמַּיִם מִשְׁפָּט
וּצְדָקָה כְּנַחַל אֵיתָן׃

But let justice roll down like waters,
and righteousness like an ever-flowing stream. (Amos 5:24)

   - "Justice" (מִשְׁפָּט) and "righteousness" (צְדָקָה) are nouns related to ideas, while "waters" (מַיִם) and "stream" (נַחַל) are things.

3. Εἰσέλθατε διὰ τῆς στενῆς πύλης· ὅτι πλατεῖα ἡ πύλη καὶ εὐρύχωρος ἡ ὁδὸς ἡ ἀπάγουσα εἰς τὴν ἀπώλειαν καὶ πολλοί εἰσιν οἱ εἰσερχόμενοι δι᾽ αὐτῆς· τί στενὴ ἡ πύλη καὶ τεθλιμμένη ἡ ὁδὸς ἡ ἀπάγουσα εἰς τὴν ζωὴν καὶ ὀλίγοι εἰσὶν οἱ εὑρίσκοντες αὐτήν.

Enter through the narrow gate; for the gate is wide and the road is easy that leads to destruction, and there are many who take it. For the gate is narrow and the road is hard that leads to life, and there are few who find it. (Matt 7:13–14)

- This verse has four nouns. "Gate" (πύλη) and "road" (ὁδὸς) are things, while "destruction" (ἀπώλειαν) and "life" (ζωὴν) are ideas.

NUMBER: Number is the grammatical category that refers to the quantity of something. In nouns, pronouns, and adjectives, number refers to whether the noun is singular or plural (or dual, in Hebrew). With verbs, number refers to whether the subject of the verb is singular or plural. See *Plural*; *Singular*.

NUMBERS: See *Cardinal number*; *Ordinal number*.

—— O ——

OBLIQUE CASE: The oblique case is any case that is not in the nominative or vocative case. See *Accusative case*; *Dative case*; *Genitive case*; *Vocative case*.

OBJECT: See *Direct object*; *Indirect object*.

OBJECT COMPLEMENT: An object complement is a word, phrase, or clause that immediately follows a direct object and completes the meaning of an expression by describing the direct object more fully. See also *Adverbial accusative*; *Direct object*.

EXAMPLES:

1. Do not consider it a hardship when you send them out from you free persons, because for six years they have given you services worth the wages of hired laborers; and the LORD your God will bless you in all that you do. (Deut 15:18)

   - The verb "consider" is followed by the direct object "it." "Hardship" is an object complement describing what exactly "it" is.

2. וַתֵּלֶד הָאִשָּׁה בֵּן וַתִּקְרָא אֶת־שְׁמוֹ שִׁמְשׁוֹן וַיִּגְדַּל הַנַּעַר וַיְבָרְכֵהוּ יְהוָה׃

The woman bore a son, and named him **Samson**. The boy grew, and the Lᴏʀᴅ blessed him. (Judg 13:24)

- The direct object of the verb "named" (lit. "called"; וַתִּקְרָא) is "him" (lit. "his name"; אֶת־שְׁמוֹ), which is then followed by the object complement, "Samson" (שִׁמְשׁוֹן), stating what he was named.

3. καὶ πάντα ὑπέταξεν ὑπὸ τοὺς πόδας αὐτοῦ καὶ αὐτὸν ἔδωκεν **κεφαλὴν** ὑπὲρ πάντα τῇ ἐκκλησίᾳ, ἥτις ἐστὶν τὸ σῶμα αὐτοῦ, τὸ πλήρωμα τοῦ τὰ πάντα ἐν πᾶσιν πληρουμένου.

And he has put all things under his feet and has made him **the head** over all things for the church, which is his body, the fullness of him who fills all in all. (Eph 1:22–23)

- The accusative noun "head" (κεφαλήν) serves as the object complement of the verb "has made" (ἔδωκεν), whose direct object is "him" (αὐτόν) by stating what he has made him.

OBJECTIVE GENITIVE: In genitive sequences in which the head noun has a verbal idea, an objective genitive receives the action of the verbal idea. For example, in the phrase "the confession of faith," "faith" is an objective genitive, as it is the thing which is being confessed. See *Genitive case.*

OBJECT PRONOUN: An object pronoun is one that is used as the object of a sentence or a prepositional phrase. Object pronouns in English are "me," "you," "her," "him," "it," "us," and "them." In Hebrew an object pronoun is suffixed to the definite direct object marker אֵת (e.g., אֹתוֹ = him). Greek object pronouns are indicated by the accusative case (e.g., αὐτήν = her).

Eₓₐₘₚₗₑₛ:

1. Cutting down the Benjaminites, they pursued **them** from Nohah and trod **them** down as far as a place east of Gibeah. (Judg 20:43)

- The pronoun "them" is used twice in this passage as an object pronoun. In the first case "them" is the direct object of the verb "pursued." In the second, "them" is the direct object of the verb "trod." The antecedent in both cases is "Benjaminites."

2. עִיר קְטַנָּה וַאֲנָשִׁים בָּהּ מְעָט וּבָא־אֵלֶיהָ מֶלֶךְ גָּדוֹל וְסָבַב **אֹתָהּ** וּבָנָה עָלֶיהָ מְצוֹדִים גְּדֹלִים:

There was a little city with few people in it. A great king came against it and besieged it, building great siegeworks against it. (Eccl 9:14)

- The direct object of the transitive verb "besieged" (סָבַב) is the object pronoun "it" (אֹתָהּ), as indicated by the definite direct object marker. Its antecedent is "city" (עִיר) a feminine singular noun.

3. ἀπέστειλεν οὖν αὐτὸν ὁ Ἅννας δεδεμένον πρὸς Καϊάφαν τὸν ἀρχιερέα.

Then Annas sent him bound to Caiaphas the high priest. (John 18:24)

- The pronoun "him" (αὐτόν) is in the accusative case and functions as the direct object of the transitive verb "sent" (ἀπέστειλεν). The antecedent of the object pronoun is Jesus from the previous verse.

OPTATIVE MOOD: Verbs in the optative mood express wish or desire. Neither English nor Hebrew have a true optative mood. English expresses wish through helping verbs, such as "may," "might," "could," "should," and "would." Hebrew verbs express wish with the cohortative (1st person), imperative (2nd person), and jussive (3rd person). Greek has four moods—indicative, imperative, optative, and subjunctive—each of which has distinct conjugations. See also *Cohortative*; *Hortatory subjunctive*; *Imperative mood*; *Jussive*; *Mood*; *Volitive*.

EXAMPLE:

1. Τί οὖν ἐροῦμεν; μὴ ἀδικία παρὰ τῷ θεῷ; μὴ γένοιτο.

What then are we to say? Is there injustice on God's part? By no means! (Rom 9:14)

- The verb γένοιτο in the phrase "by no means" is in the optative mood. With the negative particle μὴ, Paul indicates that he not even dare suggest that God commits any injustice.

ORDINAL NUMBER: Ordinal numbers are those that are used to indicate rank. In Hebrew ordinal numbers are governed by a variety of grammatical rules, depending on the value of the number. Students should consult a Hebrew grammar for those rules. Ordinal numbers in Greek decline according to gender. Masculine and neuter ordinals follow the second declension, while feminine ordinals are in the first declension.

Examples:

1. In the second year of King Darius, in the seventh month, on the twenty-first day of the month, the word of the Lord came by the prophet Haggai. (Hag 2:1)

   - The setting for Haggai's second message from the Lord is established by utilizing three ordinal numbers: "second," "seventh," and "twenty-first."

2. וְעַתָּה אֱמֶת אַגִּיד לָךְ הִנֵּה־עוֹד שְׁלֹשָׁה מְלָכִים עֹמְדִים לְפָרַס וְהָרְבִיעִי
   יַעֲשִׁיר עֹשֶׁר־גָּדוֹל מִכֹּל וּכְחֶזְקָתוֹ בְעָשְׁרוֹ יָעִיר הַכֹּל אֵת מַלְכוּת יָוָן:

   Now I will announce the truth to you. Three more kings shall arise in Persia. The fourth shall be far richer than all of them, and when he has become strong through his riches, he shall stir up all against the kingdom of Greece. (Dan 11:2)

   - The ordinal number "the fourth" (הָרְבִיעִי) indicates which of the rising kingdoms will surpass the others in the given succession of kingdoms.

3. σφοδρῶς δὲ χειμαζομένων ἡμῶν τῇ ἑξῆς ἐκβολὴν ἐποιοῦντο καὶ τῇ τρίτῃ αὐτόχειρες τὴν σκευὴν τοῦ πλοίου ἔρριψαν.

We were being pounded by the storm so violently that on the next day they began to throw the cargo overboard, and on the third day with their own hands they threw the ship's tackle overboard. (Acts 27:18–19)

- "The third" (τῇ τρίτῃ) is an ordinal number indicating which day in the sequence of harrowing events the ship's crew unloaded "the ship's tackle" (τὴν σκευὴν τοῦ πλοίου) into the sea.

—— **P** ——

PARTICIPLE: The participle is a verbal noun that behaves as a noun or adjective yet also contains a verbal action. As a noun, the participle can be translated as "the one" doing the action. As an adjective, it can function attributively or substantively. Students should consult an introductory grammar for the various nuanced uses of the participle in both Hebrew and Greek. English participles may be present tense and end in -*ing* (e.g., "burning wall"), or past and end in -*(e)n* ("risen sun"), -*ed* ("boiled meat") or -*t* ("built tower").

EXAMPLES:

1. For they have fled from the swords,
       from the drawn sword,
   from the bent bow,
       and from the stress of battle. (Isa 21:15)

   - Both "drawn" and "bent" are past participles used adjectivally to modify their respective weapons.

2.

וַיְבָרְכֵהוּ וַיֹּאמַר
בָּרוּךְ אַבְרָם לְאֵל עֶלְיוֹן
קֹנֵה שָׁמַיִם וָאָרֶץ׃

He blessed him and said,

"Blessed be Abram by God Most High,
    maker of heaven and earth" (Gen 14:19)

- The masculine singular Qal active participle "maker" (קֹנֶה) is used substantively and could be translated as "one who makes."

3. Καὶ ὅτε εἶδον αὐτόν, ἔπεσα πρὸς τοὺς πόδας αὐτοῦ ὡς νεκρός, καὶ ἔθηκεν τὴν δεξιὰν αὐτοῦ ἐπ᾽ ἐμὲ λέγων· Μὴ φοβοῦ· ἐγώ εἰμι ὁ πρῶτος καὶ ὁ ἔσχατος καὶ ὁ ζῶν, καὶ ἐγενόμην νεκρὸς καὶ ἰδοὺ ζῶν εἰμι εἰς τοὺς αἰῶνας τῶν αἰώνων καὶ ἔχω τὰς κλεῖς τοῦ θανάτου καὶ τοῦ ᾅδου.

When I saw him, I fell at his feet as though dead. But he placed his right hand on me, saying, "Do not be afraid; I am the first and the last, and the living one. I was dead, and see, I am alive forever and ever; and I have the keys of Death and of Hades." (Rev 1:17–18)

- This passage contains two participles. The first, "saying" (λέγων), is used as a present verbal idea. The second, "the living one" (ὁ ζῶν), is used substantively as a predicate nominative completing the meaning of the copula "am" (εἰμι).

PASSIVE VOICE: The passive voice of a verb is used when the subject of the verb is being acted on by an agent. Hebrew passives are represented by the Niphal, Pual, Hophal, and occasionally the Hithpael stems. The passive voice in Greek is found in each of the four moods. In some conjugations, the passive voice is indistinguishable from the middle voice. See also *Agent*; *Voice*.

EXAMPLES:

1. And when Jesus had been baptized, just as he came up from the water, suddenly the heavens were opened to him and he saw the Spirit of God descending like a dove and alighting on him. (Matt 3:16)

- In the first passive verb, the agent John acts on the subject "Jesus" when Jesus "had been baptized" (see Matt 3:14–15). In the second instance of the passive voice, "the heavens" is the subject, and they "were opened" by an anonymous agent, presumably God.

2.

לָכֵן חַכּוּ־לִי נְאֻם־יְהוָה
לְיוֹם קוּמִי לְעַד
כִּי מִשְׁפָּטִי לֶאֱסֹף גּוֹיִם
לְקָבְצִי מַמְלָכוֹת
לִשְׁפֹּךְ עֲלֵיהֶם זַעְמִי
כֹּל חֲרוֹן אַפִּי
כִּי בְּאֵשׁ קִנְאָתִי
תֵּאָכֵל כָּל־הָאָרֶץ׃

Therefore wait for me, says the Lᴏʀᴅ,
    for the day when I arise as a witness.
For my decision is to gather nations,
    to assemble kingdoms,
to pour out upon them my indignation,
    all the heat of my anger;
for in the fire of my passion
    all the earth shall be consumed. (Zeph 3:8)

- As the agent, the Lᴏʀᴅ acts upon the earth so that it "shall be consumed" (תֵּאָכֵל), appearing here in the Niphal verbal stem, which usually conveys a passive sense.

3. βλέπεις ὅτι ἡ πίστις συνήργει τοῖς ἔργοις αὐτοῦ καὶ ἐκ τῶν ἔργων ἡ πίστις ἐτελειώθη

You see that faith was active along with his works, and faith was brought to completion by the works. (Jas 2:22)

- The verb "was brought to completion" (ἐτελειώθη) is in the passive voice, indicating that "faith" (πίστις) is being acted upon by "the works" (τῶν ἔργων), the verb's agent.

PAST TENSE: The past tense refers to events that have already taken place or events that already exist relative to a fixed moment in time. In Biblical Hebrew, the past tense is generally expressed by the perfect or narrative preterite (*waw* consecutive), but it may also be expressed in other verbal forms. Greek usually expresses the past tense with the aorist, perfect, imperfect, and the pluperfect, each describing a different aspect of past time. See also *Aspect*; *Tense*.

EXAMPLES:

1. It was this Moses whom they rejected when they said, "Who made you a ruler and a judge?" and whom God now sent as both ruler and liberator through the angel who appeared to him in the bush. (Acts 7:35)

   • Each of the verbs here are in the simple past tense, indicating that the events described by them occurred prior to Stephen's speech.

2.

   וַיְדַבֵּר יְהוָה אֶל־מֹשֶׁה לֵּאמֹר:

   The LORD spoke to Moses. (Lev 17:1)

   • The Hebrew employs a narrative preterite here to express a sequential past action. Following the previous events, and prior to the writing of the passage, the LORD "spoke" (וַיְדַבֵּר).

3. Ἔπειτα μετὰ ἔτη τρία ἀνῆλθον εἰς Ἱεροσόλυμα ἱστορῆσαι Κηφᾶν καὶ ἐπέμεινα πρὸς αὐτὸν ἡμέρας δεκαπέντε

   Then after three years I did go up to Jerusalem to visit Cephas and stayed with him fifteen days. (Gal 1:18)

   • Two aorist verbs are used to express the simple past tense. First, Paul "did go" (ἀνῆλθον), which could just as easily be translated as "went." Second, Paul "stayed" (ἐπέμεινα). Both actions took place at some point in the past relative to the time he wrote the letter.

PATIENT: The noun that receives the action of a verb is known as the patient. For transitive verbs, the patient is the direct object. For passive verbs, the patient is the subject of the verb. See also *Agent*; *Direct object*; *Transitive verb*.

EXAMPLES:

1. You also, O Ethiopians,
      shall be killed by my sword. (Zeph 2:12)

- The verb "shall be killed" is passive. "Ethiopians" is the noun that receives the verb's action and is therefore its patient.

2.   נֹטֶה צָפוֹן עַל־תֹּהוּ תֹּלֶה אֶרֶץ עַל־בְּלִי־מָה׃

He stretches out Zaphon over the void,
    and hangs the earth upon nothing. (Job 26:7)

- The nouns "Zaphon" (צָפוֹן) and "earth" (אֶרֶץ) receive the action of the transitive verbs "stretches" (נֹטֶה) and "hangs" (תֹּלֶה), respectively. In this case the patient of each verb is also the direct object.

3. ἐκεῖ οὖν διὰ τὴν παρασκευὴν τῶν Ἰουδαίων, ὅτι ἐγγὺς ἦν τὸ μνημεῖον, ἔθηκαν τὸν Ἰησοῦν.

And so, because it was the Jewish day of Preparation, and the tomb was nearby, they laid Jesus there. (John 19:42)

- "Jesus" (τὸν Ἰησοῦν) receives the action of the verb "laid" (ἔθηκαν) and is the patient of the verb. Since the verb is a transitive verb, τὸν Ἰησοῦν is in the accusative case and functions as the direct object.

PERFECTIVE ASPECT: The perfective aspect is a verbal quality that describes an action that is completed. Verbs with a perfective aspect in English are formed with a conjugation of "to have" followed by a past participle (e.g., "He has studied"). In Hebrew the perfective aspect is typically expressed through the perfect tense or the narrative preterite (*waw* consecutive). Greek perfective aspect is most frequently expressed through the aorist tense and the perfect tense. Students should consult their grammar textbooks for the precise ways in which aspect can be conveyed within each language. See *Aspect*; *Perfect tense*.

PERFECT TENSE: The perfect tense is that which shows completed action. English verbs have three types of perfect tense: past perfect (e.g., "I had studied"); present perfect (e.g., "You have studied"); and future perfect (e.g., "She will have studied"). In both Hebrew and

Greek the perfect tense is a conjugated verbal form. The perfect tense in Hebrew generally expresses a simple past action, though context allows for more nuanced treatments. In Greek, grammarians have traditionally understood the Greek perfect as indicating a completed action with continuing effects or results. However, many grammarians are now arguing instead that the perfect reflects a state of being that results from a completed action. See also *Aspect*; *Perfective aspect*; *Tense*.

EXAMPLES:

1. Jesus said to him, "Go; your faith has made you well." Immediately he regained his sight and followed him on the way. (Mark 10:52)

   - Since becoming "well" has ongoing ramifications, the perfect tense "has made" is employed.

2.

   עַל נַהֲרוֹת בָּבֶל
   שָׁם יָשַׁבְנוּ גַּם־בָּכִינוּ
   בְּזָכְרֵנוּ אֶת־צִיּוֹן:

   By the rivers of Babylon—
   there we sat down and there we wept
   when we remembered Zion. (Ps 137:1)

   - The perfect verbs "sat down" (יָשַׁבְנוּ) and "wept" (בָּכִינוּ)—along with the adverb "there" (שָׁם)—express the notion that the psalmist is looking back at a time when he was in Babylon but is likely no longer in exile there. These are examples of the Hebrew perfect.

3. διότι γέγραπται· ἅγιοι ἔσεσθε, ὅτι ἐγὼ ἅγιός.

   For it is written, "You shall be holy, for I am holy." (1 Pet 1:16)

   - As is often the case when New Testament authors cite the Old Testament, the perfect is used to demonstrate the ongoing relevance of the Hebrew Scriptures. Here, "it is written" (γέγραπται) indicates that what was written in Leviticus is still applicable to the church today. Alternately, Scriptures are in a written state, as opposed to, say, an oral state.

PERSON: Person is a grammatical category used with verbs and pronouns that indicates point of view with respect to the participants in an event. Person may be first, second, or third in singular or plural. First person refers to the speaker ("I," "we"). Second person is used in direct speech and refers to the addressee ("you"). Third person refers to parties not immediately involved in a discussion ("he," "she," "it," "they"). In the biblical languages, verbs have an inherent person that matches the subject of the verb.

EXAMPLES:

1. Then I proclaimed a fast there, at the river Ahava, that we might deny ourselves before our God, to seek from him a safe journey for ourselves, our children, and all our possessions. (Ezra 8:21)

   - With the exception of "him," which is a third-person pronoun, each of the other pronouns—"I," "we," and "our"—are in the first person, as they reflect the perspective of the speaker Ezra.

2. ‏וַיִּפְקֹד דָּוִד אֶת־הָעָם אֲשֶׁר אִתּוֹ וַיָּשֶׂם עֲלֵיהֶם שָׂרֵי אֲלָפִים וְשָׂרֵי מֵאוֹת׃

   Then David mustered the men who were with him, and set over them commanders of thousands and commanders of hundreds. (2 Sam 18:1)

   - Both verbs, "mustered" (‏וַיִּפְקֹד) and "set" (‏וַיָּשֶׂם), are in the third person because their subject is "David" (‏דָּוִד). Likewise, both pronouns "him" (‏וֹ) and "them" (‏הֶם), are in the third person. That is, they are neither the ones speaking nor the ones being spoken to.

3. Εὐχαριστῶ τῷ θεῷ μου ἐπὶ πάσῃ τῇ μνείᾳ ὑμῶν

   I thank my God every time I remember you. (Phil 1:3)

   - The subject of the sentence is encoded in the verbal form "I thank" (Εὐχαριστῶ) and is in the first person since the subject is the speaker. The hearers of Paul's message are encoded in the second-person plural pronoun "you" (ὑμῶν). Incidentally, the second "I" is absent in the Greek text but is implied from context.

PERSONAL PRONOUN: See *Independent personal pronoun*.

*PHONEME: A phoneme is a minimal unit of sound in spoken language. For example, the word *cat* begins with the phoneme /k/, while the word *city* begins with the phoneme /s/.

*PHONETICS: Phonetics is the formal study of how specific speech sounds are created and perceived within a given language system.

*PHONOLOGY: Phonology is the formal study of speech sounds within a particular language system, including the sound patterns in that language.

PHRASE: A phrase is a closely related group of words functioning as a conceptual unit within a clause or sentence. There are seven types of phrases: absolute phrase; appositive phrase; gerund phrase; infinitive phrase; noun phrase; participial phrase; prepositional phrase. See *Absolute phrase*; *Apposition*; *Gerund*; *Infinitive*; *Noun*; *Participle*; *Preposition*.

PLURAL: Plural is a grammatical category indicating that there is more than one. In English, words are identified as plural by the plural -*s* suffix (singular "book"; plural "books"), or by vocabulary (singular "woman"; plural "women"). Biblical languages have morphological features that distinguish between singular and plural. Nouns, pronouns, verbs, and adjectives have an inherent number, either singular or plural (and dual in Hebrew). See also *Number*; *Singular*.

EXAMPLES:

1. He shall judge between the nations,
        and shall arbitrate for many peoples;
    they shall beat their swords into plowshares,
        and their spears into pruning hooks;
    nation shall not lift up sword against nation,
        neither shall they learn war any more. (Isa 2:4)

    • God's judgment will fall upon multiple groups, "nations" and
      "peoples." Moreover, more than one "sword," "plowshare,"
      "spear," and "pruning hook" are part of Isaiah's future vision.

2. וְכָל־הַנְּבִאִים נִבְּאִים כֵּן לֵאמֹר עֲלֵה רָמֹת גִּלְעָד וְהַצְלַח וְנָתַן יְהוָה בְּיַד הַמֶּלֶךְ׃

All the prophets were prophesying the same and saying, "Go up to Ramoth-gilead and triumph; the Lord will give it into the hand of the king." (1 Kgs 22:12)

- Multiple prophets, in fact, "all the prophets" (כָל־הַנְּבִאִים), "were prophesying" (נִבְּאִים). Therefore, both the subject and verb (in this case, a participle) are in the plural form.

3. εἶπέν τις ἐξ αὐτῶν ἴδιος αὐτῶν προφήτης
Κρῆτες ἀεὶ ψεῦσται, κακὰ θηρία, γαστέρες ἀργαί.

It was one of them, their very own prophet, who said,

"Cretans are always liars, vicious brutes, lazy gluttons." (Titus 1:12)

- Not just one Cretan, it is said, but all of the "Cretans" (Κρῆτες) are of bad reputation. Since "Cretans" is a plural noun, each of the modifiers is also plural.

PLUPERFECT TENSE: The pluperfect describes an action that is completed with reference to a previous point in time. In English the pluperfect is formed with "had" plus the past tense of a verb (e.g., "he had purchased"). Biblical Hebrew does not have a conjugated pluperfect, but a pluperfect sense may be inferred from context and translated as such. Greek has a pluperfect conjugation, though it only occurs eighty-six times in the New Testament. See also *Tense*.

Examples:

1. In this way all the work of the tabernacle of the tent of meeting was finished; the Israelites had done everything just as the Lord had commanded Moses. (Exod 39:32).

- The Israelites' work took place in the past with respect to the Lord's command, not the present situation. Hence, the use of the pluperfect is completely acceptable, as is translated here by the NRSV.

2. וַיַּעַל שִׁישַׁק מֶלֶךְ־מִצְרַיִם עַל־יְרוּשָׁלַ͏ִם וַיִּקַּח אֶת־אֹצְרוֹת בֵּית־יְהוָה וְאֶת־אֹצְרוֹת בֵּית הַמֶּלֶךְ אֶת־הַכֹּל לָקָח וַיִּקַּח אֶת־מָגִנֵּי הַזָּהָב אֲשֶׁר עָשָׂה שְׁלֹמֹה:

So King Shishak of Egypt came up against Jerusalem; he took away the treasures of the house of the Lᴏʀᴅ and the treasures of the king's house; he took everything. He also took away the shields of gold that Solomon had made. (2 Chron 12:9)

- The verb "had made" (עָשָׂה) is in the perfect conjugation. However, since the shields were made by Solomon prior to their being taken by Shishak, the pluperfect is preferred.

3. δεδώκει δὲ ὁ παραδιδοὺς αὐτὸν σύσσημον αὐτοῖς λέγων, Ὃν ἂν φιλήσω αὐτός ἐστιν, κρατήσατε αὐτὸν καὶ ἀπάγετε ἀσφαλῶς.

Now the betrayer had given them a sign, saying, "The one I will kiss is the man; arrest him and lead him away under guard." (Mark 14:44)

- Prior to the betrayal, Judas had already given "a sign" (σύσσημον); therefore, the pluperfect of the verb "had given" (δεδώκει) is appropriate.

POSSESSION: Possession refers to ownership. A noun is said to have possession of something when that thing belongs to or is controlled by the noun. In English, possession is typically expressed with -'s (or -s' for plural) following the noun that has possession, or by virtue of a possessive pronoun. In Hebrew, possession is normally expressed by virtue of the construct chain, by the use of the preposition לְ, or by a pronominal suffix. Greek generally demonstrates possession with the genitive case. See also *Genitive case*; *Possessive pronoun*.

Examples:

1. But David's men said to him, "Look, we are afraid here in Judah; how much more then if we go to Keilah against the armies of the Philistines?" (1 Sam 23:3)

- The "men" belong to David. The NRSV employs the possessive marker -'s to indicate that relationship.

2. בֶּן־אַרְבָּעִים וּשְׁתַּיִם שָׁנָה אֲחַזְיָהוּ בְמָלְכוֹ וְשָׁנָה אַחַת מָלַךְ בִּירוּשָׁלָם וְשֵׁם אִמּוֹ עֲתַלְיָהוּ בַּת־עָמְרִי׃

Ahaziah was forty-two years old when he began to reign; he reigned one year in Jerusalem. His mother's name was Athaliah, a granddaughter of Omri. (2 Chr 22:2)

- The "granddaughter" (בַּת; lit., "daughter") belongs to "Omri" (עָמְרִי). Possession is indicated here with the construct chain. Another way to translate the phrase בַּת־עָמְרִי is "Omri's granddaughter."

3. τὸ γὰρ ὄνομα τοῦ θεοῦ δι᾽ ὑμᾶς βλασφημεῖται ἐν τοῖς ἔθνεσιν, καθὼς γέγραπται.

For, as it is written, "The name of God is blasphemed among the Gentiles because of you." (Rom 2:24)

- Possession is marked by the genitive case of "God" (τοῦ θεοῦ), demonstrating God's ownership of "the name" (τὸ . . . ὄνομα). Thus, it is God's name that is blasphemed.

POSSESSIVE PRONOUN: A possessive pronoun is a word that stands in the place of a previously mentioned noun and demonstrates ownership of another noun. English possessive pronouns include "my," "mine," "your," "yours," "his," "hers," "its," "our," "ours," "their," and "theirs." Hebrew possessive pronouns are morphemes suffixed to the nouns that are possessed by the pronoun or to the preposition לְ. The Greek possessive pronouns are ἐμός (first-person singular), ἡμέτερος (first-person plural), σός (second-person singular), and ὑμέτερος (second-person plural). However, Greek more commonly articulates the possessive pronoun by placing the pronoun in the genitive case in proximity to the possessed noun. See also *Possession*.

Examples:

1. The silver is mine, and the gold is mine, says the Lord of hosts. (Hag 2:8)

   • Silver and gold belong to the Lord, according to Haggai 2:8. Since he is the speaker, these precious metals are "mine" (a use of the first common singular possessive pronoun). Incidentally, in the Hebrew text of this verse, possession is twice indicated by the preposition לְ plus the first common singular pronominal suffix.

2. וְאָהַבְתָּ אֵת יְהוָה אֱלֹהֶיךָ בְּכָל־לְבָבְךָ וּבְכָל־נַפְשְׁךָ וּבְכָל־מְאֹדֶךָ:

   You shall love the Lord your God with all your heart, and with all your soul, and with all your might. (Deut 6:5)

   • The second masculine singular possessive pronoun "your" (ךָ) identifies to whom "God" (אֱלֹהִים), "heart" (לֵב), "soul" (נֶפֶשׁ), and "might" (מְאֹד) belong.

3. Τὰ τέκνα, ὑπακούετε τοῖς γονεῦσιν ὑμῶν ἐν κυρίῳ· τοῦτο γάρ ἐστιν δίκαιον.

   Children, obey your parents in the Lord, for this is right. (Eph 6:1)

   • The second masculine plural personal pronoun "you" (ὑμῶν) is in the genitive case to indicate here possession or ownership. Another way of translating τοῖς γονεῦσιν ὑμῶν is "the parents of you." The parents belong to "you," the children who are being addressed directly.

PREDICATE: The predicate is that part of a sentence that expresses something about the subject and generally contains a verb, along with corresponding objects, complements, or adverbial modifiers. See *Finite verb*; *Nonfinite verb*.

PREDICATE ADJECTIVE: A predicate adjective is a word that ascribes a quality to a noun by equating that quality to the noun itself. In English translations the predicate adjective is used as a complement of the verb "to be." The predicate adjective in Hebrew generally precedes the noun it modifies, agrees with the noun in gender and number, but is always indefinite. In Greek, the predicate adjective comes before or after the noun and its article, but not between the noun and the article. The predicate adjective will not have an article. See also *Adjective*.

Examples:

1. But may all who seek you
       rejoice and be glad in you;
   may those who love your salvation
       say continually, "Great is the Lord!" (Ps 40:16)

   • "Great" is a predicate adjective, modifying "the Lord" and requiring the copula "is."

2. טוֹב יְהוָה לְמָעוֹז בְּיוֹם צָרָה וְיֹדֵעַ חֹסֵי בוֹ׃

   The Lord is good,
       a stronghold in a day of trouble;
   he protects those who take refuge in him. (Nah 1:7)

   • The adjective "good" (טוֹב) is a predicate adjective, modifying "the Lord" (יְהוָה). Note that the noun יְהוָה is definite, the adjective טוֹב is indefinite, and that the adjective טוֹב precedes the noun יְהוָה.

3. ὥστε ὁ μὲν νόμος ἅγιος καὶ ἡ ἐντολὴ ἁγία καὶ δικαία καὶ ἀγαθή.

   So the law is holy, and the commandment is holy and just and good. (Rom 7:12)

   • Note that the predicate adjective "holy" (ἅγιος; ἁγία) follows "the law" (ὁ ... νόμος) and "the commandment" (ἡ ἐντολή) and their respective articles, but it does not come between the article and the noun in either instance. Furthermore, the noun ἡ ἐντολή is modified by two additional predicate adjectives, "just" (δικαία) and "good" (ἀγαθή). None of the four adjectives has the article.

PREDICATE NOMINATIVE: A predicate nominative is a noun that renames the subject of the sentence. In English translations the predicate nominative is used as a complement of the verb "to be," which can logically be substituted with the word "equals." In Biblical Hebrew the predicate nominative might follow the verb "to be" (הָיָה), but more frequently it is the second noun in a verbless clause. The Greek predicate nominative often requires the linking verb "to be" (εἰμί).

Examples:

1. Whoever does not love does not know God, for God is love. (1 John 4:8)

    - The noun "love" renames the noun "God" and functions as a predicate nominative. It is important to note from this example that the copula in predicate-nominative relationships does not always imply bidirectional equality. Whereas God = love, it does not follow that love = God.

2.

    לְפָנִים הָאָרֶץ יָסַדְתָּ
    וּמַעֲשֵׂה יָדֶיךָ שָׁמָיִם:

    Long ago you laid the foundation of the earth,
      and the heavens are the work of your hands.
        (Ps 102:25 [102:26 MT])

    - The nouns "work" (מַעֲשֵׂה) and "heavens" (שָׁמָיִם) are synonymous in this passage. Since שָׁמָיִם is the second noun in the sequence in the Hebrew passage, it would be considered the predicate nominative.

3. τὰ γὰρ ὀψώνια τῆς ἁμαρτίας θάνατος, τὸ δὲ χάρισμα τοῦ θεοῦ ζωὴ αἰώνιος ἐν Χριστῷ Ἰησοῦ τῷ κυρίῳ ἡμῶν.

    For the wages of sin is death, but the free gift of God is eternal life in Christ Jesus our Lord. (Rom 6:23)

    - Both "death" (θάνατος) and "life" (ζωή) are in the nominative case and reclassify "wages" (τὰ ... ὀψώνια) and "gift" (τὸ ... χάρισμα) respectively. By using predicate nominatives, the sentence equates τὰ ὀψώνια with θάνατος, and τὸ χάρισμα with ζωή. Note that no copula verb is used in either instance.

*PREFIX: A prefix is a morpheme affixed to the beginning of a word that has a lexical meaning. Common English prefixes include *anti-*, *dis-*, *in-*, and *pre-*. Hebrew employs numerous prefixes, such as the interrogative -הֲ, the conjunctive וְ, and the inseparable prepositions בְּ, לְ, and כְּ. In Greek, the most common prefixes are the negative indicators α- (αν-), δυσ-, and νη-, the positive indicator ευ-, and prepositions that help comprise compound verbs.

PREPOSITION: A preposition is a linking word that expresses a relationship of accompaniment, agency, comparison, instrument, logic, time, or space with another element of the sentence. In Hebrew, some prepositions are always affixed to a noun, pronoun, or infinitive construct. Others are sometimes affixed, while others always stand alone. Greek prepositions mostly are single words, but several verbs take a preposition as a prefix to form a compound verb. Moreover, in Greek meaning and use of the preposition are often dictated by the case of the noun in the prepositional phrase. Prepositions have a wide and varied use in both Hebrew and Greek, and students should consult a grammar or lexicon for these nuances of meaning and function.

EXAMPLES:

1. And we have confidence in the Lord concerning you, that you are doing and will go on doing the things that we command. (2 Thess 3:4)

   • The preposition "in" expresses a relationship of accompaniment, indicating with whom the confidence resides.

2.
   מִי־אֵל כָּמוֹךָ נֹשֵׂא עָוֹן
   וְעֹבֵר עַל־פֶּשַׁע
   לִשְׁאֵרִית נַחֲלָתוֹ
   לֹא־הֶחֱזִיק לָעַד אַפּוֹ
   כִּי־חָפֵץ חֶסֶד הוּא:

Who is a God like you, pardoning iniquity
and passing over the transgression
of the remnant of your possession?
He does not retain his anger forever,
because he delights in showing clemency. (Mic 7:18)

- The inseparable preposition "like" (כְּ) is used here to convey a comparative relationship between "God" (אֵל) and "you" (ךָ-).

3. θρησκεία καθαρὰ καὶ ἀμίαντος παρὰ τῷ θεῷ καὶ πατρὶ αὕτη ἐστίν, ἐπισκέπτεσθαι ὀρφανοὺς καὶ χήρας ἐν τῇ θλίψει αὐτῶν, ἄσπιλον ἑαυτὸν τηρεῖν ἀπὸ τοῦ κόσμου.

Religion that is pure and undefiled before God, the Father, is this: to care for orphans and widows in their distress, and to keep oneself unstained by the world. (Jas 1:27)

- The first preposition, "before" (παρά), expresses a spatial relationship with respect to "God" (τῷ θεῷ). The second preposition, "in" (ἐν), could be logical (stating their condition) or temporal. The third preposition, "by" (ἀπό), indicates the agent by which one could become stained.

PRESENT TENSE: The present tense refers to an action that is concurrent with respect to a fixed point of reference, or to events that are timeless in nature. That is, the present tense is used to express what is happening now, what happens regularly, or what happens continuously. In Biblical Hebrew, the present tense may be expressed with the imperfect or, more commonly, the participle. Greek has a present-tense conjugation, but like Hebrew can also express the present with other verbal forms, including the participle. In the biblical languages, however, verbal forms sometimes referred to as *tense* more accurately refer to their *aspect*. See also *Aspect*; *Tense*.

EXAMPLES:

1. Each of you must give as you have made up your mind, not reluctantly or under compulsion, for God loves a cheerful giver. (2 Cor 9:7)

- The verb "loves" is in the present tense. That is, God's love for the giver is something that generally happens continuously.

2.   הַכְּסִיל חֹבֵק אֶת־יָדָיו וְאֹכֵל אֶת־בְּשָׂרוֹ׃

Fools fold their hands
and consume their own flesh. (Eccl 4:5)

- Two participles are used to convey the present tense: "fold" (חֹבֵק) and "consume" (אֹכֵל). As is typical with proverbs, the action of the verbs is not bound to the past or future but is habitual. These are the actions that fools typically do.

3. Ἀλήθειαν λέγω ἐν Χριστῷ, οὐ ψεύδομαι, συμμαρτυρούσης μοι τῆς συνειδήσεώς μου ἐν πνεύματι ἁγίῳ, ὅτι λύπη μοί ἐστιν μεγάλη καὶ ἀδιάλειπτος ὀδύνη τῇ καρδίᾳ μου.

I am speaking the truth in Christ—I am not lying; my conscience confirms it by the Holy Spirit—I have great sorrow and unceasing anguish in my heart. (Rom 9:1–2)

- The verbs "speaking" (λέγω), "lying" (ψεύδομαι), and "confirm" (συμμαρτυρούσης) are all conjugated as present-tense verbs. These actions were happening while Paul was writing the letter.

PROGRESSIVE TENSE: See *Imperfect tense.*

PROHIBITION: A prohibition is a negative command. That is, it commands that something be stopped or not done at all. In Hebrew the particle לֹא followed by an imperfect verb yields a general prohibition, while אַל with a second-person jussive denotes an immediate cessation of an action. Greek has several ways of depicting a negative command. Students should consult a Greek grammar for the various nuances expressed by these constructions.

Examples:

1. I hereby command you: Be strong and courageous; do not be frightened or dismayed, for the Lord your God is with you wherever you go. (Josh 1:9)

- Joshua employs a double prohibition: "do not be frightened" and "[do not be] dismayed." The negative "not" governs both verbs.

2.   וְכָל־הַשֶּׁרֶץ הַשֹּׁרֵץ עַל־הָאָרֶץ שֶׁקֶץ הוּא לֹא יֵאָכֵל:

All creatures that swarm upon the earth are detestable; they shall not be eaten. (Lev 11:41)

- The negative particle "not" (לֹא) followed by the Niphal imperfect "they shall be eaten" (יֵאָכֵל) connotes a general prohibition. That is, these particular creatures should never be eaten.

3. Οἱ πατέρες, μὴ ἐρεθίζετε τὰ τέκνα ὑμῶν, ἵνα μὴ ἀθυμῶσιν.

Fathers, do not provoke your children, or they may lose heart. (Col 3:21)

- The negative particle "not" (μὴ) followed by the present active imperative "provoke" (ἐρεθίζετε) suggests, but does not demand, that the "fathers" (οἱ πατέρες) were heretofore provoking their "children" (τέκνα) and should henceforth cease from that activity.

PRONOUN: A pronoun is a word that stands in the place of another noun or noun phrase. See also *Antecedent*; *Demonstrative pronoun*; *Independent personal pronoun*; *Interrogative pronoun*; *Intensive pronoun*; *Reflexive pronoun*; *Relative pronoun*; *Resumptive pronoun*.

PROPER NOUN: A proper noun is a name used for an individual, a geographical place name (such as a city, mountain, or river), or organization. English and Greek capitalize proper nouns. Hebrew does not have uppercase letters. See also *Noun*.

Examples:

1. Your warriors shall be shattered, O Teman,
    so that everyone from Mount Esau will be cut off. (Obad 9)

- Both "Teman" and "Mount Esau" are proper nouns referring to geographical place names synonymous with Edom.

2. וַיֵּרֹמּוּ הַכְּרוּבִים הִיא הַחַיָּה אֲשֶׁר רָאִיתִי בִּנְהַר־כְּבָר:

The cherubim rose up. These were the living creatures that I saw by the river Chebar. (Ezek 10:15)

- The "river Chebar" (נְהַר־כְּבָר) is a specifically named body of water in Mesopotamia, making it a proper noun.

3. Καὶ τῷ ἀγγέλῳ τῆς ἐν Περγάμῳ ἐκκλησίας γράψον· Τάδε λέγει ὁ ἔχων τὴν ῥομφαίαν τὴν δίστομον τὴν ὀξεῖαν ...

And to the angel of the church in Pergamum write: These are the words of him who has the sharp two-edged sword . . . (Rev 2:12)

- Since "Pergamum" (Περγάμῳ) denotes a particular city in Asia Minor, it is a proper noun. Note that the Greek text capitalizes the name of the city.

PROTASIS: In a conditional sentence, the protasis is the clause that expresses the condition and is introduced by the conjunction "if." Hebrew typically employs אִם to introduce the protasis but may use other features as well. Greek has four types of conditional sentences. First- and second-class conditions use εἰ with an indicative verb in the protasis. Third-class conditions use ἐάν followed by a subjunctive verb in the protasis. Fourth-class conditions use εἰ with the optative mood in the protasis. It should be noted that due to the decreased use of the optative mood in Hellenistic Greek, there are no complete fourth-class conditions in the New Testament. For the nuances of meaning on these conditional statements, students should consult their Greek grammar textbook. See also *Apodosis*; *Conditional sentence*.

EXAMPLES:

1. Then the LORD will establish his word that he spoke concerning me: "If your heirs take heed to their way, to walk before me in faithfulness with all their heart and with all their soul, there shall not fail you a successor on the throne of Israel." (1 Kgs 2:4)

- The protasis of the conditional sentence is introduced by the conjunction "if."

2. וְאִם־לֹא נִטְמְאָה הָאִשָּׁה וּטְהֹרָה הִוא וְנִקְּתָה וְנִזְרְעָה זָרַע׃

But **if the woman has not defiled herself and is clean**, then she shall be immune and be able to conceive children. (Num 5:28)

- The first half of the sentence, introduced by the conjunction "if" (אִם), is the protasis, establishing the condition by which the woman shall be determined innocent.

3. εἰ δέ τι ἠδίκησέν σε ἢ ὀφείλει, τοῦτο ἐμοὶ ἐλλόγα.

If he has wronged you in any way, or owes you anything, charge that to my account. (Phlm 18)

- This first-class condition begins with "if" (εἰ) at the head of the protasis, providing a situation in which Paul would reimburse Philemon.

PURPOSE CLAUSE: A purpose clause indicates the intent, goal, or aim of a particular action. English purpose clauses begin with "in order to," "in order that," "so that," "so as to," or "for the purpose of." Hebrew purpose clauses often must be inferred from context, but they are most frequently introduced with the simple וְ conjunction or the relative pronoun אֲשֶׁר. Greek purpose clauses are most often introduced by ἵνα, but ὅπως is also used with some regularity. In both biblical languages the infinitive is commonly used to convey purpose. See also *Clause*; *Subordinate clause*.

EXAMPLES:

1. And you divided the sea before them, **so that they passed through the sea on dry land**, but you threw their pursuers into the depths, like a stone into mighty waters. (Neh 9:11)

- God's intent for dividing the sea before the Israelites was "so that" they cross the sea on dry land.

2. בְּיוֹם טוֹבָה הֱיֵה בְטוֹב וּבְיוֹם רָעָה רְאֵה גַּם אֶת־זֶה לְעֻמַּת־זֶה עָשָׂה הָאֱלֹהִים עַל־דִּבְרַת שֶׁלֹּא יִמְצָא הָאָדָם אַחֲרָיו מְאוּמָה׃

In the day of prosperity be joyful, and in the day of adversity consider; God has made the one as well as the other, so that mortals may not find out anything that will come after them. (Eccl 7:14)

- The intended reason for God making both "prosperity" (טוֹבָה) and "adversity" (רָעָה) is "so that mortals may not find out anything that will come after them" (שֶׁלֹּא יִמְצָא הָאָדָם אַחֲרָיו מְאוּמָה). Note that the purpose clause is introduced by the relative שֶׁ, an alternate form of אֲשֶׁר normally associated with late Biblical Hebrew.

3. ἄρα εἰ καὶ ἔγραψα ὑμῖν, οὐχ ἕνεκεν τοῦ ἀδικήσαντος οὐδὲ ἕνεκεν τοῦ ἀδικηθέντος ἀλλ᾽ ἕνεκεν τοῦ φανερωθῆναι τὴν σπουδὴν ὑμῶν τὴν ὑπὲρ ἡμῶν πρὸς ὑμᾶς ἐνώπιον τοῦ θεοῦ.

So although I wrote to you, it was not on account of the one who did the wrong, nor on account of the one who was wronged, but in order that your zeal for us might be made known to you before God. (2 Cor 7:12)

- This passage has three purpose clauses, each introduced by the preposition ἕνεκεν, translated as "on account of" and "in order that." The first two clauses state why Paul did not write to the Corinthian church, while the third states why he did.

— Q —

QUESTION: See *Interrogative*.

— R —

REFLEXIVE PRONOUN: A reflexive pronoun functions as the direct or indirect object of a verb, in which the subject of the verb also receives the action of the verb. Examples of English reflexive pronouns include "myself," "yourself," "himself," "herself," "itself," "ourselves," "your-selves," and "themselves." Hebrew does not have any explicit reflexive pronouns. However, an English reflexive pronoun is often required when translating a passive/reflexive verbal form, when an independent personal pronoun is used for emphasis, or when a verb is followed by the preposition לְ affixed to a pronominal suffix that agrees in person, gender, and number with the verb's subject. In Greek, third-person reflexive pronouns add the prefix ἑ- to a declined αὐτός. First-person reflexive pronouns add ἐμ- to a declined αὐτός, while second-person reflexive pronouns add σέ- to a declined αὐτός in the singular. First- and second-person reflexive pronouns add ἑ- in the plural. See also *Middle voice*; *Reflexive verb*.

EXAMPLES:

1. She girds herself with strength,
   and makes her arms strong. (Prov 31:17)

   • The subject of the verb "girds" is also the direct object. That is, "herself" is the person whom "she" girds. Thus, the third feminine singular reflexive pronoun is employed.

2. וַיֹּאמְרוּ הָבָה נִבְנֶה־לָּנוּ עִיר וּמִגְדָּל וְרֹאשׁוֹ בַשָּׁמַיִם וְנַעֲשֶׂה־לָּנוּ שֵׁם
   פֶּן־נָפוּץ עַל־פְּנֵי כָל־הָאָרֶץ׃

   Then they said, "Come, let us build ourselves a city, and a tower with its top in the heavens, and let us make a name for ourselves; otherwise we shall be scattered abroad upon the face of the whole earth." (Gen 11:4)

   • The subject of the verbs "build" (נִבְנֶה) and "let us make" (נַעֲשֶׂה) is the first common plural pronoun "us," assumed by the verbal conjugation. The first common plural reflexive pronoun "ourselves" is represented by the datival use of the preposition לְ with the first common plural pronominal suffix. The phrase נִבְנֶה־לָּנוּ more formally reads, "Let us build for ourselves," and the phrase וְנַעֲשֶׂה־לָּנוּ more formally reads, "And let us make for ourselves."

3. Τοῦτο φρονεῖτε ἐν ὑμῖν ὃ καὶ ἐν Χριστῷ Ἰησοῦ,
   ὃς ἐν μορφῇ θεοῦ ὑπάρχων
   οὐχ ἁρπαγμὸν ἡγήσατο
   τὸ εἶναι ἴσα θεῷ,
   ἀλλὰ ἑαυτὸν ἐκένωσεν
   μορφὴν δούλου λαβών,
   ἐν ὁμοιώματι ἀνθρώπων γενόμενος·
   καὶ σχήματι εὑρεθεὶς ὡς ἄνθρωπος
   ἐταπείνωσεν ἑαυτὸν
   γενόμενος ὑπήκοος μέχρι θανάτου,
   θανάτου δὲ σταυροῦ.

Let the same mind be in you that was in Christ Jesus,

who, though he was in the form of God,
   did not regard equality with God
   as something to be exploited,
but emptied himself,
   taking the form of a slave,
   being born in human likeness.
And being found in human form,
   he humbled himself
   and became obedient to the point of death—
   even death on a cross. (Phil 2:5–8)

- The verbs "emptied" (ἐκένωσεν) and "humbled" (ἐταπείνωσεν) are indicative verbs. The third masculine singular reflexive pronoun "himself" (ἑαυτόν) is used in the accusative in both instances to demonstrate that the action of the verb is carried out by the same individual, "Christ Jesus" (Χριστῷ Ἰησοῦ), as the one receiving the action.

REFLEXIVE VERB: A reflexive verb is a transitive verb whose direct object is the same as the subject. Reflexive verbs in English often require a reflexive pronoun. In Hebrew the Hithpael stem often has a reflexive quality to it. The Niphal, Hophal, and Pual are sometimes used in a reflexive fashion. In Greek the reflexive idea of a verb is sometimes, though rarely, expressed with the middle voice. See also *Middle voice*; *Reflexive pronoun*.

Examples:

1. Your sun shall no more go down,

    or your moon withdraw itself;

  for the Lord will be your everlasting light,

    and your days of mourning shall be ended. (Isa 60:20)

   - The verb "withdraw" can be either transitive or intransitive. Here it is a transitive verb, meaning it requires a direct object, which in this case is "itself." The "moon" is both the subject and the object of the verb, so the verb is reflexive, and a reflexive pronoun is used to avoid the redundant and awkward "your moon withdraw your moon."

2. וַיִּסָּתֵ֨ר דָּוִ֜ד בַּשָּׂדֶ֗ה וַיְהִי֙ הַחֹ֔דֶשׁ וַיֵּ֧שֶׁב הַמֶּ֛לֶךְ עַל־הַלֶּ֖חֶם לֶאֱכֽוֹל׃

  So David hid himself in the field. When the new moon came, the king sat at the feast to eat. (1 Sam 20:24)

   - The verb "hid" (וַיִּסָּתֵר) in the Niphal can be passive or reflexive. In this case it is reflexive since "David" (דָּוִד) is both the subject and object of the verb. The NRSV captures the reflexive use by including "himself" in the translation.

3. τοὺς δὲ βεβήλους καὶ γραώδεις μύθους παραιτοῦ. γύμναζε δὲ σεαυτὸν πρὸς εὐσέβειαν.

  Have nothing to do with profane myths and old wives' tales. Train yourself in godliness. (1 Tim 4:7)

   - The verb "train" (γύμναζε) is a present active imperative. The implied subject of the imperative is the second-person pronoun "you." In this passage the direct object of the transitive verb γύμναζε is the same as the subject, that is, the one doing the training. The author uses the reflexive pronoun "yourself" (σεαυτόν) to communicate that reflexive action.

RELATIVE CLAUSE: A relative clause is a subordinate clause that modifies a noun in the main clause and is introduced by a relative pronoun. A restrictive relative clause is one that is required for the meaning of the sentence, as it provides necessary information about the noun to which it refers and is not separated by a comma. A nonrestrictive relative clause provides clarifying details regarding the noun to which it refers, but is unnecessary for the meaning of the sentence and is set off with a comma. Relative clauses are typically introduced by a relative pronoun. See also *Clause*; *Relative pronoun*.

EXAMPLES:

1. But many of the priests and Levites and heads of families, old people who had seen the first house on its foundations, wept with a loud voice when they saw this house, though many shouted aloud for joy, so that the people could not distinguish the sound of the joyful shout from the sound of the people's weeping, for the people shouted so loudly that the sound was heard far away. (Ezra 3:12–13)

   • The relative pronoun "who" introduces the restrictive relative clause "who had seen the first house on its foundations." This clause specifies which "old people" wept when they saw the new temple.

2. בָּגְדָה יְהוּדָה וְתוֹעֵבָה נֶעֶשְׂתָה בְיִשְׂרָאֵל וּבִירוּשָׁלָ͏ִם כִּי חִלֵּל יְהוּדָה קֹדֶשׁ יְהוָה אֲשֶׁר אָהֵב וּבָעַל בַּת־אֵל נֵכָר׃

   Judah has been faithless, and abomination has been committed in Israel and in Jerusalem; for Judah has profaned the sanctuary of the Lᴏʀᴅ, which he loves, and has married the daughter of a foreign god. (Mal 2:11)

   • The clause "which he loves" (אֲשֶׁר אָהֵב) is a nonrestrictive relative clause, providing important but unnecessary information regarding "the sanctuary of the Lᴏʀᴅ" (קֹדֶשׁ יְהוָה). The clause is introduced by the relative pronoun "which" (אֲשֶׁר).

3. πάλιν ἐντολὴν καινὴν γράφω ὑμῖν ὅ ἐστιν ἀληθὲς ἐν αὐτῷ καὶ ἐν ὑμῖν, ὅτι ἡ σκοτία παράγεται καὶ τὸ φῶς τὸ ἀληθινὸν ἤδη φαίνει.

Yet I am writing you a new commandment that is true in him and in you, because the darkness is passing away and the true light is already shining. (1 John 2:8)

- The relative clause "that is true in him and in you" (ὅ ἐστιν ἀληθὲς ἐν αὐτῷ καὶ ἐν ὑμῖν) is restrictive, identifying which "new commandment" (ἐντολὴν καινήν) the apostle is "writing" (γράφω). The clause is introduced by the nominative, singular, neuter relative pronoun "that" (ὅ).

RELATIVE PRONOUN: A relative pronoun is one that introduces clarifying or distinguishing information to the noun it modifies. English relative pronouns include "which," "whichever," "who," "whoever," "whom," "whomever," and "that." The most common Hebrew relative pronoun is אֲשֶׁר, although late Biblical Hebrew uses -שֶׁ, and archaic Biblical Hebrew also employs זוּ, זוֹ, and זֶה. The Greek relative pronoun is ὅς, declined according to the endings of οὗτος. See *Relative clause*.

RESTRICTIVE CLAUSE: See *Relative clause*.

RESULT CLAUSE: A result clause is one that indicates the consequence of an action. English result clauses typically begin with "so," "so that," or "such that." Hebrew result clauses are most frequently introduced with the simple וְ conjunction, but they may also be introduced by the preposition לְ or even אֲשֶׁר. Greek result clauses are often introduced by εἰς, ἵνα, ὥστε, ὥς, and ὅτι. See also *Clause*; *Subordinate clause*.

EXAMPLES:

1. For they are prophesying a lie to you, with the result that you will be removed far from your land; I will drive you out, and you will perish. (Jer 27:10)

   - The result of the false prophecies was a disinheritance of the land. The clause "with the result that you will be removed far from your land" is a result clause.

2. וַיֹּאמֶר־אֱלֹהִים לִשְׁלֹמֹה יַעַן אֲשֶׁר הָיְתָה זֹאת עִם־לְבָבֶךָ וְלֹא־שָׁאַלְתָּ
עֹשֶׁר נְכָסִים וְכָבוֹד וְאֵת נֶפֶשׁ שֹׂנְאֶיךָ וְגַם־יָמִים רַבִּים לֹא שָׁאָלְתָּ
וַתִּשְׁאַל־לְךָ חָכְמָה וּמַדָּע אֲשֶׁר תִּשְׁפּוֹט אֶת־עַמִּי אֲשֶׁר הִמְלַכְתִּיךָ עָלָיו:

God answered Solomon, "Because this was in your heart, and you have not asked for possessions, wealth, honor, or the life of those who hate you, and have not even asked for long life, but have asked for wisdom and knowledge for yourself that you may rule my people over whom I have made you king. . ." (2 Chr 1:11)

- The result of Solomon asking for "wisdom and knowledge" rather than "possessions, wealth, honor, or the life of those who hate you" is "that you may rule my people over whom I have made you king." The result clause is introduced by אֲשֶׁר.

3. Παρακαλῶ οὖν ὑμᾶς, ἀδελφοί, διὰ τῶν οἰκτιρμῶν τοῦ θεοῦ παραστῆσαι τὰ σώματα ὑμῶν θυσίαν ζῶσαν ἁγίαν εὐάρεστον τῷ θεῷ, τὴν λογικὴν λατρείαν ὑμῶν· καὶ μὴ συσχηματίζεσθε τῷ αἰῶνι τούτῳ, ἀλλὰ μεταμορφοῦσθε τῇ ἀνακαινώσει τοῦ νοὸς εἰς τὸ δοκιμάζειν ὑμᾶς τί τὸ θέλημα τοῦ θεοῦ, τὸ ἀγαθὸν καὶ εὐάρεστον καὶ τέλειον.

I appeal to you therefore, brothers and sisters, by the mercies of God, to present your bodies as a living sacrifice, holy and acceptable to God, which is your spiritual worship. Do not be conformed to this world, but be transformed by the renewing of your minds, so that you may discern what is the will of God—what is good and acceptable and perfect. (Rom 12:1–2)

- The preposition "so that" (εἰς) introduces the result clause that concludes the verse. The result of not conforming is that "you may discern what is the will of God—what is good and acceptable and perfect" (τὸ δοκιμάζειν ὑμᾶς τί τὸ θέλημα τοῦ θεοῦ, τὸ ἀγαθὸν καὶ εὐάρεστον καὶ τέλειον).

RESUMPTIVE PRONOUN: A resumptive pronoun is one that is found in a relative clause that refers to the antecedent of the relative pronoun.

In English resumptive pronouns are often rendered "in/with/by which," "in/with/by whom," and "whose." In Hebrew, resumptive pronouns are usually suffixed to a preposition or noun at the end of the relative clause. This appears to be primarily a feature of the Semitic languages (e.g., Hebrew and Aramaic), but vestiges are found in the Greek New Testament as well. See also *Relative clause*; *Relative pronoun*.

EXAMPLES:

1. Now there was a Jew in the citadel of Susa whose name was Mordecai son of Jair son of Shimei son of Kish, a Benjaminite. (Esth 2:5)

   • The Hebrew reads more woodenly, "There was a man of Judah in Susa, the citadel, and his name was Mordechai." In this sentence, the possessive pronoun "his" finds "a man of Judah" (NRSV: "a Jew") as its antecedent. The resumptive pronoun is "whose" in the NRSV.

2.
   יְהוָה סַלְעִי וּמְצוּדָתִי וּמְפַלְטִי
   אֵלִי צוּרִי אֶחֱסֶה־בּוֹ
   מָגִנִּי וְקֶרֶן־יִשְׁעִי מִשְׂגַּבִּי׃

   The LORD is my rock, my fortress, and my deliverer,
   my God, my rock in whom I take refuge,
   my shield, and the horn of my salvation, my stronghold. (Ps 18:2 [18:3 MT])

   • The third masculine singular pronominal suffix on the preposition בְּ functions as a resumptive pronoun. Translated here as "in whom" (בּוֹ), it refers back to "my God" (אֵלִי) and "my rock" (צוּרִי). A more formal translation of the second line would be, "my God, my rock, I take refuge in him."

3. ἀπεκρίνατο λέγων πᾶσιν ὁ Ἰωάννης, Ἐγὼ μὲν ὕδατι βαπτίζω ὑμᾶς· ἔρχεται δὲ ὁ ἰσχυρότερός μου, οὗ οὐκ εἰμὶ ἱκανὸς λῦσαι τὸν ἱμάντα τῶν ὑποδημάτων αὐτοῦ· αὐτὸς ὑμᾶς βαπτίσει ἐν πνεύματι ἁγίῳ καὶ πυρί.

John answered all of them by saying, "I baptize you with water; but one who is more powerful than I is coming; I am not worthy to untie the thong of his sandals. He will baptize you with the Holy Spirit and fire. (Luke 3:16)

- The pronoun "his" (αὐτοῦ) is behaving the same way it would in Hebrew at the end of a relative clause, where "sandals" (τῶν ὑποδημάτων) would have the possessive pronoun i. Another way to translate the phrase "I am not worthy to untie the thong of his sandals" (οὗ οὐκ εἰμὶ ἱκανὸς λῦσαι τὸν ἱμάντα τῶν ὑποδημάτων αὐτοῦ) is "whose sandals I am not worthy to untie."

— S —

SECOND PERSON: See *Number*; *Person*.

SENTENCE: A sentence is a syntactic unit composed of a subject and verb and contains a complete thought. The four basic types of sentences are declarative, exclamatory, imperative, and interrogative. See *Declarative sentence*; *Exclamatory sentence*; *Imperative sentence*; *Interrogative sentence*.

SINGULAR: Singular is a grammatical category related to nouns, adjectives, and verbs indicating that there is only one. In English, words are identified as singular by their lack of the plural -*s* suffix (singular "book"; plural "books"), or by vocabulary (singular "woman"; plural "women"). Biblical languages have morphological features that distinguish between singular and plural. See also *Number*; *Plural*.

EXAMPLES:

1. The elder to the beloved Gaius, whom I love in truth. (3 John 1)

   - The noun "elder" is a singular noun, indicating that the letter was addressed to one specific individual, Gaius.

2. שְׁמַע יִשְׂרָאֵל יְהוָה אֱלֹהֵינוּ יְהוָה אֶחָד:

   Hear, O Israel: The Lord is our God, the Lord alone. (Deut 6:4)

- The imperative verb "hear" (שְׁמַע) is singular, as is "Israel" (יִשְׂרָאֵל), "Lord" (יְהוָה), and "alone" (אֶחָד). Incidentally, the noun God (אֱלֹהִים) is morphologically plural and can refer to either plural "gods" or to the singular God of Israel. When the latter, אֱלֹהִים takes a singular verb.

3. ὅς ἐστιν εἰκὼν τοῦ θεοῦ τοῦ ἀοράτου, πρωτότοκος πάσης κτίσεως, ὅτι ἐν αὐτῷ ἐκτίσθη τὰ πάντα ἐν τοῖς οὐρανοῖς καὶ ἐπὶ τῆς γῆς, τὰ ὁρατὰ καὶ τὰ ἀόρατα, εἴτε θρόνοι εἴτε κυριότητες εἴτε ἀρχαὶ εἴτε ἐξουσίαι· τὰ πάντα δι' αὐτοῦ καὶ εἰς αὐτὸν ἔκτισται.

He is the image of the invisible God, the firstborn of all creation; for in him all things in heaven and on earth were created, things visible and invisible, whether thrones or dominions or rulers or powers—all things have been created through him and for him. (Col 1:15–16)

- This passage illustrates how number pertains to verbs, nouns, and adjectives. The verb "is" (ἐστιν) is a third-person singular verb. The noun "image" (εἰκών) is nominative, feminine, singular. The adjective "invisible" (ἀοράτου) is masculine, genitive, singular.

STATIVE VERB: A stative verb is one that expresses a state of being rather than an action. Stative verbs are used in the context of attitude, being, cognition, emotion, perception, and stance. Hebrew stative verbs have a distinct conjugation in the third masculine singular perfect, following the vowel pattern in כָּבֵד as an example.

EXAMPLES:

1. I know, however, that the king of Egypt will not let you go unless compelled by a mighty hand. (Exod 3:19)

- To "know" is to be in a state of having knowledge, so the verb "know" is a stative verb.

2. וַיֻּגַּד לִשְׁלֹמֹה לֵאמֹר הִנֵּה אֲדֹנִיָּהוּ יָרֵא אֶת־הַמֶּלֶךְ שְׁלֹמֹה וְהִנֵּה אָחַז בְּקַרְנוֹת הַמִּזְבֵּחַ לֵאמֹר יִשָּׁבַע־לִי כַיּוֹם הַמֶּלֶךְ שְׁלֹמֹה אִם־יָמִית אֶת־עַבְדּוֹ בֶּחָרֶב׃

Solomon was informed, "Adonijah is afraid of King Solomon; see, he has laid hold of the horns of the altar, saying, 'Let King Solomon swear to me first that he will not kill his servant with the sword.'" (1 Kgs 1:51)

- The verb "is afraid" (יָרֵא) is a third masculine singular Qal perfect with the distinctive stative verb vocalization. "Adonijah" (אֲדֹנִיָּהוּ) is in a state of being afraid.

3. εἰ ἐν τῇ ζωῇ ταύτῃ ἐν Χριστῷ ἠλπικότες ἐσμὲν μόνον, ἐλεεινότεροι πάντων ἀνθρώπων ἐσμέν.

If for this life only we have hoped in Christ, we are of all people most to be pitied. (1 Cor 15:19)

- The verb "to hope" is one that expresses either attitude or emotion. The aorist perfect participle translated as "have hoped" (ἠλπικότες) expresses the notion of having a hopeful state of being.

SUBJECT COMPLEMENT: A complement is a word, phrase, or clause that completes the meaning of an expression. A subject complement follows the verb and provides additional information regarding the subject. There are two types of subject complements: predicate adjective and predicate nominative. See *Predicate adjective*; *Predicate nominative*.

SUBJECTIVE GENITIVE: In genitive sequences in which the head noun carries a verbal idea, a subjective genitive performs the action of the verbal idea. For example, in the phrase "the revelation of God," "God" is a subjective genitive, as God is the one who does the revealing. See *Genitive case*.

SUBJUNCTIVE MOOD: The subjunctive mood expresses potentiality or possibility. Verbs in the subjunctive mood are often translated with "may" or "might." Clauses containing a subjunctive verb often begin with "if." Although Hebrew does not have moods, context sometimes suggests that a verb is best translated as a subjunctive. The Greek subjunctive is identifiable by its morphological features. See also *Mood*.

Examples:

1. Then the captain on whose hand the king leaned said to the man of God, "Even if the Lord were to make windows in the sky, could such a thing happen?" But he said, "You shall see it with your own eyes, but you shall not eat from it." (2 Kgs 7:2)

   • Since the making of windows is only a potentiality or possibility, the verb "were" is in the subjunctive mood.

2.

לוּ־אִישׁ הֹלֵךְ רוּחַ וָשֶׁקֶר כִּזֵּב
אַטִּף לְךָ לַיַּיִן וְלַשֵּׁכָר
וְהָיָה מַטִּיף הָעָם הַזֶּה:

   If someone were to go about uttering empty falsehoods,
   saying, "I will preach to you of wine and strong drink,"
   such a one would be the preacher for this people! (Mic 2:11)

   • The Qal active participle translated "were to go about" (הֹלֵךְ) is expressed in the subjunctive mood because it is governed by the particle "if" (לוּ), which denotes an expression of wish or potentiality.

3. ἀλλὰ διὰ τοῦτο ἠλεήθην, ἵνα ἐν ἐμοὶ πρώτῳ ἐνδείξηται Χριστὸς Ἰησοῦς τὴν ἅπασαν μακροθυμίαν πρὸς ὑποτύπωσιν τῶν μελλόντων πιστεύειν ἐπ' αὐτῷ εἰς ζωὴν αἰώνιον.

   But for that very reason I received mercy, so that in me, as the foremost, Jesus Christ might display the utmost patience, making me an example to those who would come to believe in him for eternal life. (1 Tim 1:16)

   • The verb "might show" (ἐνδείξηται) is in the subjunctive mood, expressing the potentiality of the "patience" of Jesus. Note also that the subjunctive is here indicated with the morpheme -η- as a connecting vowel.

SUBORDINATE CLAUSE: A subordinate clause is one that supports and modifies an independent clause. A subordinate clause is dependent on the main clause and cannot stand alone. See also *Clause*; *Causal* *clause; Conditional clause; Epexegetical clause; Purpose clause; Result clause; Temporal clause.*

EXAMPLES:

1. As morning appeared, the woman came and fell down at the door of the man's house where her master was, until it was light. (Judg 19:26)

   - The subordinate clause "as morning appeared" is an adverbial temporal clause providing the setting for when "the woman came."

2. וַיִּירְאוּ הָאֲנָשִׁים יִרְאָה גְדוֹלָה וַיֹּאמְרוּ אֵלָיו מַה־זֹּאת עָשִׂיתָ כִּי־יָדְעוּ הָאֲנָשִׁים כִּי־מִלִּפְנֵי יְהוָה הוּא בֹרֵחַ כִּי הִגִּיד לָהֶם:

   Then the men were even more afraid, and said to him, "What is this that you have done!" For the men knew that he was fleeing from the presence of the LORD, because he had told them so. (Jonah 1:10)

   - The final clause, "because he had told them so" (כִּי הִגִּיד לָהֶם) is a causal subordinate clause. The rest of that final sentence is an independent clause that could stand alone without it.

3. ἀπάτωρ ἀμήτωρ ἀγενεαλόγητος, μήτε ἀρχὴν ἡμερῶν μήτε ζωῆς τέλος ἔχων, ἀφωμοιωμένος δὲ τῷ υἱῷ τοῦ θεοῦ, μένει ἱερεὺς εἰς τὸ διηνεκές.

   Without father, without mother, without genealogy, having neither beginning of days nor end of life, but resembling the Son of God, he remains a priest forever. (Heb 7:3)

   - The main sentence is "he remains a priest forever" (μένει ἱερεὺς εἰς τὸ διηνεκές). Everything leading up to this is a subordinate clause modifying "priest" (ἱερεύς).

SUBORDINATING CONJUNCTION: See *Conjunction.*

SUBSTANTIVAL ADJECTIVE: A substantival adjective is one that behaves as a noun. Some substantival adjectives are used either with great regularity or almost exclusively as substantives (e.g., "the rich," "the

sinners"). In both Hebrew and Greek, substantival adjectives generally take the article.

EXAMPLES:

1. Your glory, O Israel, lies slain upon your high places!
   How the mighty have fallen! (2 Sam 1:19)

   • The subject of the verb "have fallen" is the plural adjective "the
     mighty." Therefore, "the mighty" is a substantival adjective.

2. וְנַסְתֶּם גֵּיא־הָרַי כִּי־יַגִּיעַ גֵּי־הָרִים אֶל־אָצַל וְנַסְתֶּם כַּאֲשֶׁר נַסְתֶּם מִפְּנֵי
   הָרַעַשׁ בִּימֵי עֻזִּיָּה מֶלֶךְ־יְהוּדָה וּבָא יְהוָה אֱלֹהַי כָּל־קְדֹשִׁים עִמָּךְ:

   And you shall flee by the valley of the LORD's mountain, for the valley
   between the mountains shall reach to Azal; and you shall flee as you fled
   from the earthquake in the days of King Uzziah of Judah. Then the LORD my
   God will come, and all the holy ones with him. (Zech 14:5)

   • The "holy ones" (קְדֹשִׁים) is a masculine plural adjective func-
     tioning as the second subject of the verb "will come" (בָּא),
     which is gapped from the main clause.

3. τότε οἱ δίκαιοι ἐκλάμψουσιν ὡς ὁ ἥλιος ἐν τῇ βασιλείᾳ τοῦ
   πατρὸς αὐτῶν. ὁ ἔχων ὦτα ἀκουέτω.

   Then the righteous will shine like the sun in the kingdom of their Father.
   Let anyone with ears listen! (Matt 13:43)

   • The subject of the first sentence in this verse is the adjective
     "the righteous" (οἱ δίκαιοι), which is in the nominative case.
     As the subject of the verb "will shine" (ἐκλάμψουσιν), it func-
     tions as a substantival adjective.

*SUFFIX: A suffix is a lexically valued morpheme affixed to the end
of a word. Some examples of English suffixes are *-ed*, *-ing*, and *-ly*.
Suffixes in Hebrew include the directional הָ-, the paragogic ן-, and
the enclitic ם-, to name a few. A few of the many Greek suffixes
include -πλασιων, -τος, and -ως.

SUPERLATIVE: A superlative is a qualitative assessment of one item among all other items in a given category. English superlatives are generally marked by the suffix -*est* on the quantifying adjective (e.g., smart*est*). Hebrew marks superlatives in several ways. The most common constructions are as follows: (1) the comparative מִן prefixed to the word כָּל־ (= "more than all"); (2) the placement of a noun in construct with the same noun (e.g., שִׁיר הַשִּׁירִים = "the song of songs" = "the greatest song"); (3) repetition of words (e.g., קָדוֹשׁ קָדוֹשׁ קָדוֹשׁ = "holy, holy, holy" = most holy"). Greek superlatives are marked with the suffixes -τατος (-τατη, -τατον) and -ιστος (-ιστη, -ιστον), as well there being a few specific vocabulary items that denote a superlative notion. There are a few additional rules for Greek superlatives for which students should consult their grammar textbook.

EXAMPLES:

1. For from the least to the greatest of them,
      everyone is greedy for unjust gain;
   and from prophet to priest,
      everyone deals falsely. (Jer 6:13)

   • Both "least" and "greatest" are superlatives, conveying the idea that nothing lies beyond either of these two extremes. This expression also forms a hendiadys, denoting not just the extremes but everything in between.

2. כִּי כֹה אָמַר אֲדֹנָי יְהוִה הִנְנִי מֵבִיא אֶל־צֹר נְבוּכַדְרֶאאצַּר מֶלֶךְ־בָּבֶל
   מִצָּפוֹן מֶלֶךְ מְלָכִים בְּסוּס וּבְרֶכֶב וּבְפָרָשִׁים וְקָהָל וְעַם־רָב:

   For thus says the Lord GOD: I will bring against Tyre from the north King Nebuchadrezzar of Babylon, king of kings, together with horses, chariots, cavalry, and a great and powerful army. (Ezek 26:7)

   • The phrase "king of kings" (מֶלֶךְ מְלָכִים) is asserting that, as king of Babylon, which was the most powerful empire in the ancient Near East during the time of Ezekiel, Nebuchadnezzar is the greatest king. This is an example of a Hebrew superlative.

3. οἱ δὲ ἐσιώπων· πρὸς ἀλλήλους γὰρ διελέχθησαν ἐν τῇ ὁδῷ τίς μείζων.

But they were silent, for on the way they had argued with one another who was the greatest. (Mark 9:34)

- The adjective "greatest" (μείζων) is the comparative form of the adjective "great" (μέγας). Since the comparison is made among all disciples in the group, it functions here as a superlative. There is one disciple whose greatness (however they defined it) supersedes the greatness of all the others.

*SYLLABLE: A syllable is the smallest unit of pronunciation in a word, consisting of one and only one vowel sound.

SYNDETIC CONSTRUCTION: A syndetic construction is a syntactic feature in which two elements sharing syntactic roles in a sentence are joined by a conjunction. When multiple units are joined together, it is called a polysendetic construction. See also *Asyndetic construction*.

EXAMPLES:

1. Greet Prisca and Aquila, who work with me in Christ Jesus, and who risked their necks for my life, to whom not only I give thanks, but also all the churches of the Gentiles. (Rom 16:3–4)

- The nouns "Prisca" and "Aquila" are joined by the conjunction "and." They are thus said to be in syndetic relationship with one another.

2. וָאֶשָּׂא אֶת־עֵינַי וָאֵרֶא וְהִנֵּה אַרְבַּע קְרָנוֹת:

And I looked up and saw four horns. (Zech 2:1)

- The expressions "I looked up" (lit. "I lifted my eyes"; וָאֶשָּׂא אֶת־עֵינַי) and "saw" (וָאֵרֶא) comprise a syndetic construction, connoting the same idea and occupying the same semantic category in the sentence, and are joined by the conjunction "and" (וְ).

3. καὶ ἐγένετο φωνὴ πρὸς αὐτόν, Ἀναστάς, Πέτρε, θῦσον καὶ φάγε.

Then he heard a voice saying, "Get up, Peter; kill and eat." (Acts 10:13)

- The verbs "kill" (θῦσον) and "eat" (φάγε) are joined by the conjunction "and" (καί). These two verbs share the syntactic role of commands given to Peter.

*SYNTAX: Syntax refers to the logical arrangement and sequence of words, phrases, and clauses in a sentence.

—— T ——

TELIC CLAUSE: See *Result clause*.

TELIC VERB: See *Aktionsart*.

TEMPORAL CLAUSE: A temporal clause is a type of subordinate clause that indicates the time of an event presented in the independent clause. Temporal clauses may include an absolute timeframe (e.g., "noon," "month of Nisan"), or they may be relative to surrounding events in the narrative (e.g., "before," "on the eighth day"). See also *Clause*; *Subordinate clause*.

EXAMPLES:

1. When he had taken the scroll, the four living creatures and the twenty-four elders fell before the Lamb, each holding a harp and golden bowls full of incense, which are the prayers of the saints. (Rev 5:8)

   - The temporal clause "when he had taken the scroll" sets the scene for the time in which the creatures and elders fell before the Lamb.

2. וַיְהִי דְבַר־יְהוָה אֶל־יִרְמְיָה אַחֲרֵי שְׁבוֹר חֲנַנְיָה הַנָּבִיא אֶת־הַמּוֹטָה מֵעַל צַוַּאר יִרְמְיָה הַנָּבִיא לֵאמֹר:

   Sometime after the prophet Hananiah had broken the yoke from the neck of the prophet Jeremiah, the word of the LORD came to Jeremiah. (Jer 28:12)

- "Sometime after the prophet Hananiah had broken the yoke from the neck of the prophet Jeremiah" (אַחֲרֵי שְׁבוֹר חֲנַנְיָה הַנָּבִיא אֶת־הַמּוֹטָה מֵעַל צַוַּאר יִרְמְיָה הַנָּבִיא) is a temporal clause denoting when "the word of the LORD came to Jeremiah" (וַיְהִי דְבַר־יְהוָה אֶל־יִרְמְיָה). Note that in the Hebrew text the temporal clause follows the independent clause.

3. Καὶ εὐθὺς ἔτι αὐτοῦ λαλοῦντος παραγίνεται Ἰούδας εἷς τῶν δώδεκα καὶ μετ᾽ αὐτοῦ ὄχλος μετὰ μαχαιρῶν καὶ ξύλων παρὰ τῶν ἀρχιερέων καὶ τῶν γραμματέων καὶ τῶν πρεσβυτέρων.

   Immediately, while he was still speaking, Judas, one of the twelve, arrived; and with him there was a crowd with swords and clubs, from the chief priests, the scribes, and the elders. (Mark 14:43)

   - The clause, "immediately, while he was still speaking" (καὶ εὐθὺς ἔτι αὐτοῦ λαλοῦντος) is a temporal clause, stating when Judas arrived relative to the time Jesus was talking.

TENSE: The tense of a verb refers to the time and duration of its action. In English, *tense* most commonly refers to the time of an event. In the biblical languages, however, verbal forms sometimes referred to as *tense* more accurately refer to its *aspect*. See *Aspect*; *Future tense*; *Imperfect tense*; *Past tense*; *Perfect tense*; *Pluperfect tense*; *Present tense*.

THIRD PERSON: See *Number*; *Person*.

TRANSITIVE VERB: A transitive verb is a finite verb that takes a direct object. See also *Direct object*; *Finite verb*.

EXAMPLES:

1. Then Boaz took ten men of the elders of the city, and said, "Sit down here"; so they sat down. (Ruth 4:2)

   - The verb "took" is a transitive verb, requiring the direct object "ten men" to complete the thought.

2. וַיַּעֲלֶה עָמְרִי וְכָל־יִשְׂרָאֵל עִמּוֹ מִגִּבְּתוֹן וַיָּצֻרוּ עַל־תִּרְצָה:

So Omri went up from Gibbethon, and all Israel with him, and they besieged Tirzah. (1 Kgs 16:17)

- The verb "besieged" (וַיָּצֻרוּ) is a transitive verb, with its direct object being "Tirzah" (תִּרְצָה).

3. Λέγω οὖν, μὴ ἀπώσατο ὁ θεὸς τὸν λαὸν αὐτοῦ; μὴ γένοιτο· καὶ γὰρ ἐγὼ Ἰσραηλίτης εἰμί, ἐκ σπέρματος Ἀβραάμ, φυλῆς Βενιαμίν.

I ask, then, has God rejected his people? By no means! I myself am an Israelite, a descendant of Abraham, a member of the tribe of Benjamin. (Rom 11:1)

- The verb "rejected" (ἀπώσατο) requires a direct object, which, in this case, is "his people" (τὸν λαὸν αὐτοῦ). Therefore, ἀπώσατο is a transitive verb.

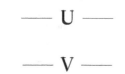

— U —

— V —

VERB: See *Finite verb*; *Nonfinite verb*; *Predicate*.

VOCATIVE CASE: The vocative case is the case used in direct address. As with other cases, Hebrew does not have the vocative case, while Greek does, though some grammarians dispute that it is distinct from the nominative case. English translations often render the vocative by setting apart the addressee with commas and/or placing "O" before the addressee. See also *Case*; *Nominative case*.

EXAMPLES:

1. I said, "O Lᴏʀᴅ God of heaven, the great and awesome God who keeps covenant and steadfast love with those who love him and keep his commandments . . ." (Neh 1:5)

- Nehemiah addresses God directly in his prayer, so "Lᴏʀᴅ" functions as a vocative case noun.

2.

אֵיךְ נָפַלְתָּ מִשָּׁמַיִם
הֵילֵל בֶּן־שָׁחַר
נִגְדַּעְתָּ לָאָרֶץ
חוֹלֵשׁ עַל־גּוֹיִם׃

How you are fallen from heaven,
   O Day Star, son of Dawn!
How you are cut down to the ground,
   you who laid the nations low! (Isa 14:12)

- The prophet mocks the king of Babylon and addresses him here as "Day Star" (הֵילֵל), which functions as a noun in the vocative case.

3. ὁ δὲ Παῦλος, Οὐ μαίνομαι, φησίν, κράτιστε Φῆστε, ἀλλὰ ἀληθείας καὶ σωφροσύνης ῥήματα ἀποφθέγγομαι.

But Paul said, "I am not out of my mind, most excellent Festus, but I am speaking the sober truth." (Acts 26:25)

- The noun "Festus" (Φῆστε), along with its modifying adjective "most excellent" (κράτιστε), are both in the vocative case, as Paul is speaking directly to Festus.

VOICE: Voice is a verbal characteristic that represents the relationship between the subject and the verb. See *Active voice*; *Middle voice*; *Passive voice*.

VOLITIVE: A volitive is a verb that expresses wish or desire on the part of the speaker. Hebrew has three types of volitives: cohortative (first person); imperative (second person), and jussive (third person). Greek volitives can be expressed by the future indicative (imperatival future), the imperative, and the subjunctive. See *Cohortative*; *Imperative mood*; *Imperative sentence*; *Jussive*; *Hortatory subjunctive*; *Optative mood*; *Subjunctive mood*.

WISH CLAUSE: See *Volitive*.

RESOURCES FOR FURTHER STUDY

HEBREW GRAMMAR COMPANIONS

Long, Gary A. *Grammatical Concepts 101 for Biblical Hebrew.*
2nd ed. Grand Rapids: Baker Academic, 2013.

Murphy, Todd J. *Pocket Dictionary for the Study of Biblical Hebrew.*
IVP Pocket Reference Series. Downers Grove, IL: IVP
Academic, 2003.

Van Pelt, Miles V. *English Grammar to Ace Biblical Hebrew.* Grand
Rapids: Zondervan, 2010.

Williams, Michael. *The Biblical Hebrew Companion for Bible
Software Users: Grammatical Terms Explained for Exegesis.*
Grand Rapids: Zondervan, 2015.

GREEK GRAMMAR COMPANIONS

DeMoss, Matthew S. *Pocket Dictionary for the Study of New
Testament Greek.* IVP Pocket Reference Series. Downers Grove,
IL: IVP Academic, 2001.

Lamerson, Samuel. *English Grammar to Ace New Testament Greek.*
Grand Rapids: Zondervan, 2004.

Long, Gary A. *Grammatical Concepts 101 for Biblical Greek: Learning Biblical Greek Grammatical Concepts through English Grammar*. Grand Rapids: Baker Academic, 2006.

Strauss, Mark L. *The Biblical Greek Companion for Bible Software Users: Grammatical Terms Explained for Exegesis*. Grand Rapids: Zondervan, 2016.

BEGINNING HEBREW GRAMMARS

Cook, John A., and Robert D. Holmstedt. *Beginning Biblical Hebrew: A Grammar and Illustrated Reader*. Grand Rapids: Baker Academic, 2013.

Hackett, Jo Ann. *A Basic Introduction to Biblical Hebrew*. Peabody, MA: Hendrickson, 2010.

Kutz, Karl V., and Rebekah Josberger. *Learning Biblical Hebrew: Reading for Comprehension: An Introductory Grammar*. Bellingham, WA: Lexham, 2018.

Pratico, Gary D., and Miles V. Van Pelt. *Basics of Biblical Hebrew Grammar*. 3rd ed. Grand Rapids: Zondervan, 2019.

Ross, Allen P. *Introducing Biblical Hebrew*. Grand Rapids: Baker Academic, 2001.

Seow, Choon-Leong. *A Grammar for Biblical Hebrew*. Rev. ed. Nashville: Abingdon, 1995.

BEGINNING GREEK GRAMMARS

Black, David Alan. *Learn to Read New Testament Greek*. 3rd ed. Nashville: Broadman & Holman, 2009.

Decker, Rodney J. *Reading Koine Greek: An Introduction and Integrated Workbook*. Grand Rapids: Baker Academic, 2014.

Gibson, Richard J., and Constantine R. Campbell. *Reading Biblical Greek: A Grammar for Students*. Grand Rapids: Zondervan, 2017.

Mounce, William D. *Basics of Biblical Greek Grammar*. 4th ed. Grand Rapids: Zondervan, 2018.

Porter, Stanley E., Jeffrey T. Reed, and Matthew Brook O'Donnell. *Fundamentals of New Testament Greek*. Grand Rapids: Eerdmans, 2010.

Schwandt, John D. *An Introduction to Biblical Greek: A Complete Introductory Grammar That Builds on a Classic Approach to Learning Greek*. Bellingham, WA: Lexham, 2017.

Intermediate Hebrew Grammars

Arnold, Bill T., and John H. Choi. *A Guide to Biblical Hebrew Syntax*. 2nd ed. Cambridge: Cambridge University Press, 2018.

Fuller, Russell T., and Kyoungwon Choi. *Invitation to Biblical Hebrew Syntax: An Intermediate Grammar*. Invitation to Theological Studies. Grand Rapids: Kregel Academic, 2017.

Reymond, Eric D. *Intermediate Biblical Hebrew Grammar: A Student's Guide to Phonology and Morphology*. Atlanta: SBL, 2018.

Intermediate Greek Grammars

Köstenberger, Andreas J., Benjamin L. Merkle, and Robert L. Plummer. *Going Deeper with New Testament Greek: An Intermediate Study of the Grammar and Syntax of the New Testament*. Nashville: Broadman & Holman, 2016.

Mathewson, David L., and Elodie Ballantine Emig. *Intermediate Greek Grammar: Syntax for Students of the New Testament*. Grand Rapids: Baker Academic, 2016.

Wallace, Daniel B. *Greek Grammar Beyond the Basics: An Exegetical Syntax of the New Testament*. Grand Rapids: Zondervan, 1996.

HEBREW REFERENCE GRAMMARS

Gesenius, Wilhelm, E. Kautzsch, and A. E. Cowley. *Gesenius'
    Hebrew Grammar*. Oxford: Clarendon, 1910.
Joüon, Paul. *A Grammar of Biblical Hebrew*. Translated by
    T. Murako. Subsidia Biblica 27. Third reprint of the second ed.,
    with corr. Rome: Gregorian & Biblical Press, 2006.
Van der Merwe, Christo, Jacobus A. Naudé, and Jan H. Kroeze.
    A Biblical Hebrew Reference Grammar. 2nd ed. London:
    Bloomsbury, 2017.
Waltke, Bruce K., and Michael O'Connor. *An Introduction to
    Biblical Hebrew Syntax*. Winona Lake, IN: Eisenbrauns, 1990.

GREEK REFERENCE GRAMMARS

Blass, F., A. Debrunner, and Robert W. Funk. *A Greek Grammar of
    the New Testament and Other Early Christian Literature*. Rev. ed.
    Chicago: University of Chicago Press, 1961.
Robertson, A. T. *A Grammar of the Greek New Testament in
    the Light of Historical Research*. 3rd ed. London: Hodder &
    Stoughton, 1914.
Smyth, Herbert W. *Greek Grammar*. Cambridge: Harvard
    University Press, 1966.

SCRIPTURE INDEX

An Interpretive Lexicon of New Testament Greek

G. K. Beale, Daniel J. Brendsel, and William A. Ross

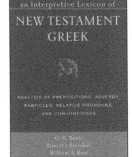

This revolutionary new aid for students of New Testament Greek functions both as a lexicon and as an interpretive handbook. It lists most Greek prepositions, adverbs, particles, relative pronouns, conjunctions, and other connecting words that are notorious for being some of the most difficult words to translate. For each word included, page references are given for several major lexical resources where the user can go to examine the nuances and parameters of the word for translation options, saving the translator considerable time.

This lexicon adds an interpretive element for each word by categorizing its semantic range into defined logical relationships. This interpretive feature of the book is tremendously helpful for the exegetical process, helping the translator to closely follow the logical flow of the text. *An Interpretive Lexicon of New Testament Greek* is thus a remarkable resource for student, pastor, and scholar alike.

Available in stores and online!

Biblical Hebrew Vocabulary in Context

Miles V. Van Pelt and Gary D. Pratico

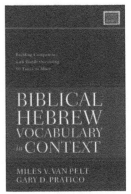

A practical resource for biblical Hebrew students, *Biblical Hebrew Vocabulary in Context* strengthens and reinforces vocabulary by helping students to read words that occur fifty times or more in the context of the Hebrew Bible. All 642 of these Hebrew words have been collated into 195 verses and/or verse fragments in order to help students practice and retain their Hebrew vocabulary.

Biblical Hebrew Vocabulary in Context includes two primary sections:

- Section one allows students to write their own glosses, parse verbs, or note issues related to grammar and syntax. An English translation is also provided in this first section.
- Section two provides the same biblical verses from the first section but with minimal room for notes and without an English translation.

Available in stores and online!